# WHEN THE NATURAL
## MEETS THE
# SUPERNATURAL

# WHEN THE MEETS THE NATURAL SUPERNATURAL

*Discovering the Person and Work of the Holy Spirit*

# CHRIS SUSTAR

Editor: Lance Colkmire
Editorial Assistant: Tammy Hatfield
Copy Editor: Esther Metaxas
Technical Design: R. Ariel Vázquez

**ISBN: 978-1-59684-866-5**

Copyright © 2015 by Pathway Press
1080 Montgomery Avenue
Cleveland, Tennessee 37311

Visit *www.pathwaypress.org* for more information.

Printed in the United States of America

To my wife,
Leah,
and my sons,
Jaren and Evan

# CONTENTS

# INTRODUCTION

THE YEAR WAS 1949. A young woman named Francis walked into the Hoskins Avenue Church of God in Charlotte, North Carolina. Her husband was the pastor, and the church was in revival. It was winter, and the outside temperature was cold. In those days, there was no central heating. Instead, the sanctuary had a potbelly stove that burned coal to keep out the chill.

On this particular night, as the service progressed, Francis felt the presence of God surge within her spirit. The Holy Spirit moved on her, and she began to speak in tongues. Suddenly, she walked over to the stove. A fire raged inside the black heater, and the door was glowing hot. She grabbed the handle and swung open the door. Those sitting closest to the stove immediately felt a rush of heat.

To everyone's amazement, Francis reached in the door with both hands. Someone let out a scream, but it didn't faze her. She scooped up two handfuls of red-hot coals and walked around the church. By this time, the power of God was being manifested throughout the congregation. She returned to the stove, threw in the coals, and returned to her seat. Several people came over right away to check her hands. There was no sign of burns!

Some unbelievers attended the service that night, and they were amazed by what they witnessed. God used that miracle to reveal His glory and to convict them of their sins. Before the service ended, they rushed to the altar and gave their lives to Jesus Christ.

A fairy tale, you say? A made-up story? Nope. That event really happened. I should know: Francis was my grand-mother! I loved Mammaw Gosnell dearly, and I was very close to her. She was a godly woman full of the Holy Spir-it. She exemplified what it meant to live in the presence and power of the Holy Spirit.

The Holy Spirit is God's gift of Himself to you. He longs to be involved in every aspect of your life, and that is possible through the ever-abiding presence of His Spirit. Without Him, my grandmother's experience would be a fascinating but far-fetched story. With Him, you have the potential to tell your own stories, as you personally experience His power and glory!

The prologue, "Who Is the Holy Spirit?", is a primer on the person of the Holy Spirit. Call it "Holy Spirit 101," if you like. The remainder of the book is divided into three sections. Section I explores the Holy Spirit's role in salvation. In soteriology (the doctrine of salvation), the major emphasis is generally on Jesus and His work. While Jesus is the center and source of your redemption, the Holy Spirit brings conviction of sins, dwells in your heart at salvation, and places you into the body of Christ.

Section II deals with the Spirit's ability to give you victory over your flesh and to enable you to live a holy, obedient life. You'll learn how to be led by the Spirit and what it means to bear the fruit of the Spirit. We'll explore how He can cause you to shine with the glory of Jesus!

In Section III, you will discover that God's supernatural power is available to you through the baptism with the Holy Spirit. We will explore speaking in tongues and investigate the gifts of the Spirit. You will get a better understanding of why Spirit-filled people act the way they do when they encounter the supernatural power of God.

I've written this book because I want to help you learn how to walk and live in the Spirit. I want you to experience the dynamics of the Spirit-filled life. Without the Holy Spirit, Christianity is an empty religion. If your version of Christianity is dry, powerless, and ineffective, you have a spiritual problem. The Holy Spirit is the answer to your problem! He is the life of the Church, and He is the life of the believer. If you are desperate for a source of spiritual vitality, you have all you need in the person and work of the Holy Spirit.

# WHO IS THE HOLY SPIRIT?

A FARMER SENT HIS SON TO COLLEGE to earn a horticultural degree in order to eventually help his father work the farm. His son attended the first semester and returned home with a change of mind. He told his father, "I don't want to study horticulture anymore; I want to study medicine."

"Medicine?" his father asked.

"Yes," replied his son. "I want to be an obstetrician."

The father said, "A what?"

The son repeated, "An obstetrician, Dad."

His father said, "No sir! No son of mine is going to be an obstetrician!"

In frustration, the young man cried, "But Dad, why not?"

The farmer replied, "You'll go get a degree in medicine and become an obstetrician. Then, somebody will come along and find a cure, and you'll be out of a job!"

Unfortunately, when it comes to the topic of the Holy Spirit, many are like the farmer. We really don't know that much about Him. One of the great problems in the church today is that God the Holy Spirit is not given His proper place, nor is His ministry on our behalf understood. The late Ray H. Hughes, former Church of God general overseer, said, "There is such an appalling lack of knowledge concerning the Holy Ghost and His ministry that He has been referred to as the 'Unknown Person of the Godhead'" (*Who Is the Holy Ghost?*).

Most believers have a good working knowledge and a developed theology concerning God the Father and God the Son, but they are ignorant of the Holy Spirit. Francis Chan writes: "From my perspective, the Holy Spirit is tragically neglected and, for all practical purposes, forgotten. While no evangelical would deny His existence, I'm willing to believe there are millions of churchgoers across America who cannot confidently say they have experienced His presence or action in their lives over the past year. And many of them do not believe they can" (*Forgotten God*).

Individuals with a non-Pentecostal background or those who were not raised in church may say, like the believers at Ephesus in Acts 19:2, "We have not so much as heard whether there is a Holy Spirit." Let's explore the question, "Who is the Holy Spirit?"

## The Holy Spirit Is a Person

If you are sitting in a room with others, you are in a room with *persons*. You can get up, walk over, and interact with any one of them. I want you to see the Holy Spirit in the same way. He is a person with whom you can interact. I want to be clear: He is not an "it." Many mistakenly refer to the Holy Spirit in this way. Never refer to Him as "it." Refer to your spouse as "it" for a few days and see how that works out for you!

In the Bible, the Holy Spirit is never called "it"; He is referred to as "He." He is not an influence, a power, a manifestation, a blessing, a feeling, an emanation, a divine energy or force, or an impersonal object—He is a person. In John 14:15-17, Jesus affirms the Spirit's personality, ascribing personal characteristics to Him. He calls Him a *Helper*, the *Spirit of truth*, One who *abides* and *dwells*, and One who can be *known*. He speaks of Him with personal pronouns.

The Holy Spirit has the exclusive characteristics of a person. First, He has a *mind*. In Romans 8:27, Paul refers to the "mind of the Spirit." He thinks, rationalizes, judges, deems, considers, and makes value decisions. In 1 Corinthians 2:10-11, Paul says, "For the Spirit searches all things, yes, the deep things of God. . . . Even so no one knows the things of God except the Spirit of God."

Second, He has *emotions*, which means He has feelings. In Ephesians 4:30, we are told He can be grieved. Have you ever been upset? Has anyone ever upset you so badly that it hurt your heart? The Holy Spirit can have His heart hurt through our disobedience and rebellion. In Romans 15:30, Paul mentions "the love of the Spirit." He can love and can be loved. The love of God is poured into our hearts by the Holy Spirit. I'm grateful for the assurance that no one loves me like the Spirit loves me!

Third, He has a *will*. In Acts 16, Paul and his companions wanted to go to the northern part of what is modern-day Turkey to preach the gospel. The Holy Spirit, however, would not permit them to travel there. Instead, through a vision given to Paul, the Spirit sent them to Macedonia in Greece. Did you know there are things the Holy Spirit wants for you? There are things the Spirit wants you to do, and there are activities He doesn't want you to get involved in. There are places the Holy Spirit wants to send you, and there are places where He does not want you to go. If you will listen to the Holy Spirit, you can know the mind of God and you can walk in His will!

## The Holy Spirit Is a Divine Person

In Acts 5:3-4, the Holy Spirit is called "God." In 2 Corinthians 3:18, He is called "Lord." In the fourth century AD, certain men in the Church conjured up the idea that God the Father created the Spirit. This idea made the Holy Spirit less than God, and that is not true. God the Holy Spirit is one with God and one with the Godhead—co-equal, co-eternal, and con-substantial with the Father and the Son.

We believe in one God, but He has revealed Himself as a Trinity (there is one God with three personas). The Trinity is a holy mystery that must be embraced by faith. Many times, I heard my dad say, "If you try to figure out the Trinity, it will blow your mind. If you don't believe it, it will blow your soul." Christianity fully rejects polytheism, and Christians do not worship three gods. Deuteronomy 6:4 reads, "Hear, O Israel: The Lord our God, the Lord is one!" Yet, from Genesis to Revelation, God has revealed that within that oneness, or unity, there is a tri-unity of God the Father, God the Son, and God the Holy Spirit. Also, the order of the Godhead does not imply superiority or inferiority. Just because the Holy Spirit is listed last does not mean He is inferior to the Father or the Son. He is as much divine as the Father and the Son are divine.

As you accept the Holy Spirit as a divine person, you should strive to be holistic in your worship. What I am about to say may upset your theology. For years, I was comfortable with worshiping God the Father and God the Son. One day, someone said to me, "You need to be comfortable in worshiping God the Holy Spirit. He is God, too, you know!"

I took those words to heart and, in time, I started worshiping the Holy Spirit. I want to challenge you to offer praise and worship to the Spirit of God. Say something like this: "Holy Spirit, I love You. I worship You as God, and I thank You for all that You are doing in me and through me."

While this may be a major adjustment for some believers, it is not as foreign an idea as you may think. How often has a congregation sang "The Doxology" in church and never realized what they were singing? "Praise God, from whom all blessings flow;/Praise Him, all creatures here below;/Praise Him above ye heavenly host;/Praise Father, Son, and *Holy Ghost*." Even the popular Doxology encourages you to praise the Holy Spirit!

Because He is a divine person, He has divine attributes. He is called the "eternal Spirit" in Hebrews 9:14. From everlasting to everlasting, the Holy Spirit is God. He is *all-powerful*. He is *Creator*. In Genesis 1, He is bringing order from chaos and creating all that exists. He is *all-knowing*.

The Spirit of God is *omnipresent*. David writes: "Where can I go from Your Spirit? Or where can I flee from Your presence? If I ascend into heaven, You are there; if I make my bed in hell, behold, You are there. If I take the wings of the morning, and dwell in the uttermost parts of the sea, even there Your hand shall lead me, and Your right hand shall hold me" (Ps. 139:7-10).

Wherever you can go, the Holy Spirit will be there. There is no situation you can find yourself in that God is absent. He is there when the devil is giving you grief, when the hordes of hell are breathing down the back of your neck, when someone is persecuting you for your faith, and when you do not feel like He is anywhere to be found. He is a "very present help in trouble" (Ps. 46:1).

When you mess up, He is there. When you think no one is looking, He is there. When you think the preacher will never discover what you are doing, He is there. I am glad for the ever-abiding presence of the Spirit of God!

His ability to raise the dead serves as evidence of His divinity. Only God can raise the dead! On that first Easter Sunday morning, it was the Holy Spirit who resurrected Jesus from the grave in newness of life. Romans 8:11 says, "If the Spirit of Him who raised Jesus from the dead dwells in you, He who raised Christ from the dead will also give life to your mortal bodies through His Spirit who dwells in you." One day, "the Lord Himself will descend from heaven with a shout, with the voice of an archangel, and with the trumpet of God. And the dead in Christ will rise" from their state of death by the resurrection power of the Holy Spirit (1 Thess. 4:16). He will give life, immortality, and incorruptibility to those who have died in the Lord.

## The Importance of Seeing the Holy Spirit as a Divine Person

If you are going to live a full, fruitful, and spiritual life as a child of God, it is essential that you know the Holy Spirit and His relationship to you. The Christian life is meant to be lived in the Spirit. You cannot be a genuine follower of Jesus without Him. If you have been transformed by the saving power of Jesus' death on the cross, you are dependent on the presence and power of the Holy Spirit. Consequently, you must become familiar and comfortable with Him and His work in your life. You must learn to walk in Him and experience the fullness of His efforts on your behalf. God has a Spirit-filled life planned for you, and He wants you totally surrendered to His Spirit. As you get to know Him, your spiritual life will be divinely animated and anointed. This is the era of the Holy Spirit, and God wants you walking and living in His Spirit—not just getting a tingly touch on Sunday morning or running to Him when you are in trouble.

Why have so many failed to understand the Spirit? One reason is *the devil*. He is the enemy of your soul, and he does not want you to see the Holy Spirit correctly. He wants you to ignore the Holy Spirit or treat Him as an impersonal force or feeling. He will do all he can by diabolical means to get you to discount the Holy Spirit as a *Person*—as Someone to be known, talked to, heard from, and empowered by. If you find yourself resisting the Holy Spirit and His work in you, step back and take a good look at yourself. Is it possible that the Enemy has a stronghold in your mind?

The other reason many do not experientially know the Spirit involves *irresponsible churches and leaders*. Unfortunately, while many have been taught about God the Father and God the Son, they have heard little or nothing about God the Holy Spirit. It is as if their church and its leaders have said, "Holy Spirit, we believe in You, but we don't know what to do with You. Please go over there in a corner and sit. We want You in the church, but we will tell You when we need You." Sunday after Sunday, people are exiting church buildings saying, "Won't somebody tell me about the Holy Spirit and how He relates to my life?"

When I was growing up in church, we sang a song titled "To Be Like Jesus." While I did not care much for the song (it was slow and boring to a little boy), its message was profound. God's goal for you is to be "conformed to the image" of your divine brother, Jesus (Rom. 8:29). This amazing goal is attained only by the presence and the power of the Holy Spirit in you. Jesus tried His best to convey this truth to His disciples just before He went to the cross. In John 14:16, He promised that the Father would send "another Helper"—someone different yet similar in nature to Jesus. Of course, He was referring to the Holy Spirit.

Let me illustrate from the natural. If you have a red apple and a red tomato, they are different in nature, even though they share the same color. However, if you have a green apple and a red apple, they are similar in nature, even though they have different tints in their skins. Jesus wanted His followers to grasp the fact that the Holy Spirit was *His* Spirit. This is why, in the Bible, He is often called the "Spirit of Jesus" or the "Spirit of Christ."

After His death and resurrection, Jesus was returning to heaven, and He knew the thought of His absence would devastate the apostles. He wanted to assure them that things were going to be all right. Actually, He wanted to assure them that things were going to be even better. Why? Trapped in a human body, He was limited by time and space. He could only be at one place at one time, externally influencing and engaging people. If He left and put His Spirit in His followers, He could live in every believer—everywhere, at all times!

If you were a member of my congregation, and we spent time together every day, we could talk about the Lord and the Bible. I could influence you in your spiritual life up to a point.

Realistically, it would not be possible for me to be with you every moment of every day. What if you could put the spirit of me inside of you (scary thought, isn't it)? When you had a spiritual question, I would be right there to answer it. When you faced a temptation, I would be present to convince you to make a right moral decision. When you caught a 25-pound striped bass or received a pay raise at your job, I would be there to rejoice with you. I would be with you all the time to help you. In time, because of my presence and influence, you would even start thinking, talking, and acting like me.

In the new covenant, Jesus' promise in John 14 is now a reality. Through the gift of salvation, you are a recipient of the Spirit of Jesus! Because His Holy Spirit lives inside of you, you have access to Jesus twenty-four hours a day, seven days a week. When you are down, His Spirit encourages you. When you are tempted, He helps you find a way of escape. When you sin, He convicts you. When you do not feel saved, He assures you that you are still God's child. When you do not know how to pray, He helps you say the right words.

I want to challenge you to do four things:

1. See the Holy Spirit as a Person.

2. Talk to Him in prayer.

3. Praise and worship Him.

4. Ask Him for spiritual help when you need it.

In essence, I'm challenging you to become aware of His presence inside of you and begin to engage Him. Starting now, make it your life's goal to get to know the *Person* of the Holy Spirit!

# Section I
## Salvation and the Spirit

## THE HOLY SPIRIT
## AND THE SINNER

THE PRINCIPAL WORK OF THE HOLY SPIRIT in relation to an unsaved person is *conviction*. Every individual born into this world is born in sin. He or she is born with a sin nature and with a penchant to sin. Every person who lives and matures eventually develops a lifestyle or a practice of sin. The Bible makes it clear that sin separates an individual from God, creating a chasm that only Jesus Christ can span. Consequently, every person is born in need of a savior. Everyone needs reconciliation to God through Jesus. Thus, it is the work of the Holy Spirit to convict men and women of their sins and to bring them to a place of repentance and salvation.

Speaking of the Holy Spirit, the Lord said, "And when He has come, He will convict the world of sin, and of righteousness, and of judgment: of sin, because they do not believe in Me; of righteousness, because I go to My Father and you see Me no more; of judgment, because the ruler of this world is judged" (John 16:8-11). Jesus said He would send the Holy Spirit in this era of the new covenant to convict the world of sin, righteousness, and judgment. What exactly does that mean?

To *convict* means "to confute or to overwhelm in an argument." Have you ever been so wrong in an argument that winning was not possible? Have you ever been so wrong and the other person so right that you knew it was a losing battle? This is how the Holy Spirit works with a sinner. He tells him or her, "You can argue with Me all day long why you should stay in sin, but I have multiple counter-arguments for every argument you have. I am going to overwhelm you with evidence to show you that you are not supposed to be in sin!" Of course, no sinner has ever won an argument with God!

Another meaning for *convict* is "to admonish or to express disapproval of in a gentle, earnest, or solicitous manner." This means the Spirit approaches the sinner and says, "I don't like what you are doing! This is unacceptable to Me, and you cannot keep going in this direction. Something has to change!" His approach is gentle but consistent. He will never force anyone to be saved, but He is passionate in His dealings with the sinner. Unashamedly, He solicits the sinner to leave the life of sin and come to Christ.

## The Spirit Convicts the World of Sin

The Holy Spirit convicts *individuals* of their sins. He rebukes people for acts of sin such as lying, cheating, and stealing. Jesus, however, said the Holy Spirit convicts the entire *world* of the sin of unbelief ("They do not believe in Me").

A vast majority of the American population believes in the existence of God. Many affirm Jesus' existence as a historical figure, and most have a general understanding of the Ten Commandments. Yet, millions of Americans continue to live sinfully and refuse to accept God's wonderful gift of salvation.

My uncle, Bob Sustar, preached a sermon titled, "Missing Heaven by Eighteen Inches." The distance from the top of your head to the bottom of your heart is approximately a foot and a half. Many people have a head knowledge of God, but what they profess has never been transferred to their heart. In Romans 10:9-10, Paul writes, "If you confess with your mouth the Lord Jesus and believe in your heart that God has raised Him from the dead, you will be saved. For with the heart one believes unto righteousness, and with the mouth confession is made unto salvation."

Claiming to believe in Jesus and His moral law will never make you right with God. God makes it clear that the only way to be reconciled to Him is "by grace . . . through faith" in the person and work of Jesus Christ (Eph. 2:8). Faith is believing in the death, burial, and resurrection of Jesus and trusting Him alone to forgive your sin and give you eternal life. The Holy Spirit continually works to persuade people to stop sinning and put their hope in Jesus as the answer to their sin problem.

## The Spirit Convicts the World of Righteousness

Jesus is the Righteous One, and no sin can be found in Him. On earth, He always fulfilled God's will, and was constantly living to please His Father. Obviously, He could do this because He was God, and God can do no wrong. Jesus, however, was both God and man. In the Incarnation, humanity was added to His divinity, making Him 100 percent God and 100 percent man. He fought the devil, resisted the influence of a sinful world, and battled the desires of His own flesh. As the God-man, Jesus modeled for us how to live righteously in a human body in a sinful world controlled by a wicked devil. The Holy Spirit's role is to convince sinful men and women that, through Jesus, they can be saved and can live right. He persuades unbelievers that it is possible to overcome sin and temptation and, like Jesus did, obey God's moral standard.

Satan blinds people so they cannot see the truth. Consequently, they say things like, "I'm too bad. God can't save me. You don't know what I've said and done." They feel hopeless and helpless. So, the Holy Spirit comes along and says, "Don't listen to the devil. There is hope for you! You can be saved . . . you can be righteous . . . you can be changed . . . you can be like Jesus!" He tells the sinner, "Where sin abounded, grace abounded much more" (Rom. 5:20). The good news of the Gospel is, it does not matter how bad you have been: God can reach you right where you are. God has delivered people from a drunken stupor and a drug-induced state and saved them. I have pastored people who were a mess when God came to them. They will tell you that the words of an old song best describe their moment of salvation: "When my Savior reached down for me / When He reached way down for me / I was lost and undone without God or His Son / When He reached down His hand for me."

The Lord may have to reach way down for a sinner, but He will never say, "I'm sorry. I can't reach you; I can't get to you." You may be at the bottom looking up, but the Holy Spirit will convince you that God can rescue you from your pit of sin and cleanse you. He will say, "The blood of Jesus can reach you; God's grace can reach you; His mercy can reach you."

Growing up, we would sing, "There's power, power, wonder-working power in the blood of the Lamb." The Holy Spirit tells the sinner, "You aren't a hopeless case. There's still power in the blood of Jesus. 'Would you be free from your burden of sin? . . . Would you o'er evil a victory win? There's wonderful power in the blood!'"

## The Spirit Convicts the World of Judgment

A scary and sad truth is that every person is born under judgment. Sin condemns us, and punishment of the worst kind awaits us. The Bible warns "the wages of sin is death" (Rom. 6:23) and "the soul who sins shall die" (Ezek. 18:4). This death is more than *physical* death; everyone, both good and bad, will die some day. This is *spiritual* death, where an individual is eternally separated from God, His presence, and the possibility of redemption. No more goosebumps while in church, no more conviction while hearing an anointed message. Because of sin, all are born on death row, destined for hell. So, the Holy Spirit comes to argue with and admonish the sinner over his or her impending doom.

Yet, Jesus points out there is another who is under the judgment of God. He identifies the devil as "the ruler of this world" (John 12:31; 16:11). What is the connection between his condemnation and the sinner's condemnation? Satan is the embodiment of sin, rebellion, and pure iniquity. There is no redemption for the devil, and he is destined for hell. Jesus made it clear that hell is "prepared for the devil and his [fallen] angels" (Matt. 25:41). The atoning work of Jesus on the cross cannot save the devil. However, the Holy Spirit says to the sinner, "You are condemned, and you are on the road to hell to be punished for your sin. But while there is no redemption for the devil, I have good news: redemption is available to you! You can be pardoned. Jesus took your punishment on the cross, and heaven can be your home. You can experience eternal life right now through Jesus Christ!"

This freedom from judgment for our sins is the essence of John 3:16-17: "For God so loved the world that He gave His only begotten Son, that whoever believes in Him should not perish but have everlasting life. For God did not send His Son into the world to condemn the world, but that the world through Him might be saved." God's Spirit wants every sinner to know "there is no more condemnation for those who are in Christ Jesus, who do not walk after the flesh but after the Spirit!" (see Rom. 8:1).

## Conviction by the Holy Spirit Is Unpleasant but Necessary

I once told my wife, "As a preacher and pastor, I have to say some hard and straight things to people. But if I don't say those things, who will?" Occasionally, I have to get one-on-one with people and have hard conversations concerning sin or unacceptable behavior. It is not that I enjoy doing this, but it is part of my calling as a minister of the gospel and as a spiritual leader in His church.

Before I planted our church in Anderson, I was an associate pastor at Praise Cathedral Church of God in Greer, South Carolina. Our lead pastor scheduled an evangelist that had never been to our church, and no staff members were familiar with his ministry. The first service was on Sunday morning. When the evangelist came to the pulpit, he started promoting his products. Next, he started tossing recordings of his sermons to the crowd. Then, he threw Christian T-shirts to the congregation. The church leaders, including the lead pastor, were in shock. Finally, he received his own offering without asking permission!

After lunch, my pastor brought him into his office and confronted him. I will never forget his opening statement to the evangelist: "Son, I'm going to say to your face what pastors say behind your back after you leave their churches." With love and spiritual authority, he admonished that young man for his behavior. He gave him strict guidelines on what he could and could not do while ministering in his pulpit. Finally, he encouraged the evangelist to discontinue the "gimmicks" and preach the Word. Unfortunately, while the young preacher obeyed my pastor's directives for the week, he continued his antics at his next revival.

The Holy Spirit says hard, straight things to a sinner that no one else is saying. Generally, sinners accept and endorse other sinners' activity. More and more in America, our government is legislating immorality and making sin legal. While others condone or approve one's sin, the Spirit of God convicts the sinful heart and reveals the consequences of sin. Why? He wants to convince the transgressor to receive salvation and to be free from the bondage of sin. Conviction may hurt. It may make you mad or sad, but the Holy Spirit is speaking words in love that will ultimately bring life and freedom.

Through conviction, the Holy Spirit generates *godly sorrow* within the sinner. Second Corinthians 7:10 proclaims, "For godly sorrow produces repentance leading to salvation." The Spirit's conviction touches both the mind and the heart. Like the Prodigal Son in Luke 15, the sinner will come to his senses. Like the crowd on the Day of Pentecost in Acts 2, he or she will be cut to the heart, crying, "What should I do? I can't go on like this any longer! Something has to change!"

I'm convinced a sinner under conviction who is repenting and coming to Jesus for salvation will experience some emotions. The sinner will feel deep remorse for his or her sinful life and ungodly ways. Their heart will be stirred or broken, and they will be sorry enough that they will choose to change.

I look for humility, desperation, and sincerity when a sinner comes to Christ. Hot tears streaming down a man's face indicate godly sorrow that is leading him to a place of repentance and salvation. However, when the blood is applied, forgiveness is granted, redemption occurs, and all sins are washed away, the godly sorrow is replaced with unspeakable joy! Peace like a river floods the soul, and the love of God fills the heart. Tears give way to laughter and a lasting smile. When someone asks, "What happened to you?" the newborn person can reply, "Jesus just came into my life and saved me from my sin!"

## The Power of Conviction

Words at the foot of an infidel's deathbed read, "God is nowhere." His little daughter came in, and he asked her to read it to him. She read the words this way: "God is *now here*." Suddenly, the father's eyes filled with tears. He felt himself a lost sinner in the presence of God. That is *conviction*.

Many years ago, there was a worldly woman who had a godly servant. Night after night, she remained awake until four or five o'clock in the morning, waiting for her mistress to return from a night of partying. Night after night, her mistress found her reading the Bible. One evening, the mistress came in and looked over the servant's shoulder, saying, "What melancholy stuff are you reading this time?" However, in that moment, her eye caught the word *eternity*, and suddenly the laugh was changed to a strange feeling of sadness. Sleep fled from her eyes and laughter from her heart, and the word *eternity* haunted her. With sorrow and in desperation, she surrendered her life to Christ. That is *conviction*.

A poor woman was in great distress because she could not pay her rent. She expected someone to come, seize her personal property, and eject her from her home. Her pastor heard of her trouble and came to her house with the money for her rent. He knocked, but he could not get an answer. He tapped on all the doors and windows, so eager to help her, but he received no response. Finally, he left, carrying the money with him. The poor woman, however, was at home the entire time. She thought it was someone seeking entrance to carry away her possessions in lieu of the rent. She had tightly locked every door and window and ignored the pastor's knocking.

Sadly, many people are like that poor woman. The Holy Spirit comes with conviction, knocking at their heart's door, and they fear it is God coming to take away everything when, in fact, He has come to give them just what they need!

## Born of the Spirit

The heartbeat of God is to radically transform sinners into believers and followers of Jesus Christ. He desires to change the sinner's status from a spiritually lifeless enemy of God to a child of the living God. The Lord desperately wants to give unsaved men and women a "do-over"—a second chance at life by removing sin and reconciling them to Himself through Jesus Christ. This change God produces in a repentant sinner is so radical that it is called a "new birth."

In John 3, Jesus has a discussion with a Jewish leader, Nicodemus. The Lord insists to him, "You must be born again" (v. 7). The word *again* can also be translated "from above." So, Jesus could have said, "You must be born from above." He was conveying to Nicodemus, and to us, that a spiritual new birth is the work of God.

This truth is important, because many falsely believe that someone or something other than God can improve their spiritual condition. No one or nothing, however, can save you from your sinful state other than God. No amount of counseling, reformation, or psychiatric help can fix your sin problem. You cannot save yourself. Good works, charitable giving, self-help programs, and hours of volunteering given to good causes cannot make you right with God. It is only when you surrender your heart and life to God's saving initiative through Jesus that you are born again, or born from above.

What does it mean to experience a new birth? The idea is beginning life all over again. In 1 Peter 2:2, converts to Christ are called "newborn babes." When you are born again, you experience a new sphere of spiritual life—you "enter the kingdom of God" (John 3:5). It is a dynamic change involving a drastic break with sin and the impartation of spiritual life. You become spiritually alive!

## The New Birth Is Effected by the Holy Spirit

God created the family, and fundamentally it consists of a father, a mother, and a child (or children). Through procreation, a father and mother produce offspring through natural birth. What is true in the natural is also true in the spiritual. The Bible reveals God as the Father—the Creator (or Progenitor) of all humanity, and especially of those who are saved. This is why we pray, "Our Father in heaven, hallowed be Your name" (Matt. 6:9). The Bible also reveals God as the Son. He is the "only begotten Son" (John 3:16), in whom the Father is "well pleased" (Matt. 17:5) and who is "the firstborn" among all who are saved from their sins (Rom. 8:29). Jesus is the older brother of every born-again child of God.

The Bible also reveals God as the Holy Spirit. While God never calls Himself "God the Mother" in the Bible, He does convey an image of the Holy Spirit as One who operates maternally in a spiritual sense, giving the repentant sinner a new birth. The Spirit of God is the divine agent of regeneration, the One who creates and imparts new life into a person at the moment of salvation. In 2 Corinthians 5:17, Paul writes, "Therefore, if anyone is in Christ, he is a new creation; old things have passed away; behold, all things have become new." Just as a newborn baby is a new creation, the individual who is born of the Spirit is a new creation in Jesus Christ.

Second Peter 1:4 says God has given us His Word, filled with "exceedingly great and precious promises." Through these promises, we become "partakers of the divine nature." When you were naturally born, you became a partaker of human nature. As a result, you look, act, and react as a human being, according to your human nature. Unfortunately, human nature is corrupted by sin, so how you behave and speak is often sinful. However, when you are born again, you become a partaker of the divine nature. Through regeneration, you demonstrate God's nature. You look, act, react, and speak like Jesus, reflecting His character.

If you are saved, something about you should make people think about Jesus. Something about the way you conduct yourself, about the way you deal with trouble or suffering, should make them think of the God within you. Sure, you will not always get it right. Living for Jesus is a process, and each day you are becoming more like Jesus. Like the song says, "Jesus on the inside working on the outside. Oh, what a change in my life!"

## Profound and Mysterious

Jesus told Nicodemus, "The wind blows where it wishes, and you hear the sound of it, but cannot tell where it comes from and where it goes. So is everyone who is born of the Spirit" (John 3:8). We can see the effects of the wind without seeing the wind itself. It may uproot trees or blow gently on our face, but we never see it. We do not know where it comes from or where it is going.

The same is true of the Holy Spirit. I never know where He is coming from or where He is going. I do not fully comprehend His work in regeneration. I do not understand how He can take a vile, mean, selfish man or woman and change them through the power of regeneration. I cannot grasp how He is changing me, giving me a new nature, making me a new creation, and giving me a fresh start. However, I experience and know the effects of His wonderful work in my life every day!

The new birth radically transforms an individual in regard to sin, righteousness, and personal relationships. From the book of 1 John, here are four effects of the wind of the Spirit:

- A born-again person will love God and keep His commandments (5:2-3).

- A born-again person will not continue sinning or practicing sin (3:9).

- A born-again person will overcome the world (5:4-5).

- A born-again person will have a genuine Christian love for others (4:7-8).

The new birth is the start of a new life. Because of a new nature, you will obey God and deny sin any place in your life. You will push back against rather than cave in to the pressure of this sinful world system. You will genuinely care for people and respond to them with acts and words of compassion. You will love people you really do not like! There is a song that sums it up so well: "I just started living. I found me a brand-new life."

Here is my challenge to you:

- If you are not saved, yield to the Holy Spirit's conviction. Give your life to Jesus and accept God's free gift of salvation by faith.

- If you are saved, worship the Holy Spirit and offer Him gratitude for His convicting work in your life.

# THE HOLY SPIRIT IN ME

WHEN YOU ARE SAVED, (1) the Holy Spirit takes up residence inside your body; and (2) God assumes ownership of your body and your spirit.

## The Holy Spirit Takes Up Residence

All born-again believers are indwelt by the Holy Spirit. In Romans 8:9, Paul asserts, "You are not in the flesh but in the Spirit, if indeed the Spirit of God dwells in you. Now if anyone does not have the Spirit of Christ, he is not His." Anyone who is born-again has the Holy Spirit, and anyone who is not born-again does not have the Holy Spirit. Put differently, anyone who has the Holy Spirit within is a redeemed Christian, while anyone who does not have the Holy Spirit is not a redeemed believer. You may call yourself a Christian, join a church, and serve in that church; but if you do not have the Holy Spirit living inside of you, you are not a born-again believer.

Having the Holy Spirit inside of you is really having Jesus Christ within you. In the above verse, the Holy Spirit is called the "Spirit of Christ." The intimate connection between God the Son and God the Holy Spirit is evident in the Bible. For example, numerous times in the New Testament, we are told that Jesus is seated presently at the right hand of God in heaven. When Stephen, the first martyr of the church, was being stoned to death, he saw a vision of Jesus and cried, "I see the heavens opened and the Son of Man standing at the right hand of God!" (Acts 7:56). Yet, in Ephesians 3:17, Paul prays that Christ would dwell in the heart of every believer.

How can Jesus be seated in heaven and live in every believer's heart simultaneously? By His Holy Spirit, Jesus lives inside of every believer. This is true because, at the moment of your salvation, you experience a spiritual union with Jesus.

In 1 Corinthians 5, Paul rebukes the Corinthian church for tolerating a sexually immoral man in the congregation. In chapter 6, he points out that sexual immorality is an important and dangerous sin because it involves the union of two bodies into one flesh—something that God preserved for marriage alone. Paul takes that physical concept and makes a correlating spiritual truth: When a believer is joined to the Lord at the moment of the new birth, he or she is one spirit with Him. The redeemed man or woman is joined spiritually with Jesus.

If you have been born again, you and Jesus are one in spirit through the union of your spirit with His Holy Spirit. Why is this so important? Everywhere you go and whatever you do, Jesus is there with you by His Spirit. Every time you do right, Jesus is there. When you choose to do wrong, Jesus is there. If you decide to commit sin, you indirectly involve Jesus in your immorality! This should be unthinkable to you, and this should serve as an inhibitor to sinning.

Because your spirit is joined to the Holy Spirit, your body is His temple. A temple is a house of worship—a sacred place for holy purposes. It is the house of God and the place where He deals with people. In the Old Testament, King Solomon built a magnificent temple in the city of Jerusalem. Doubtless, some Israelites mistakenly believed that God lived at their temple. In reality, God simply met with men and women there as they offered sacrifices and worshiped Him. Solomon understood this, saying, "Behold, heaven and the heaven of heavens cannot contain You. How much less this temple which I have built!" (2 Chron. 6:18).

In the New Testament, however, God has chosen to take up permanent residence inside the temple (body) of every born-again believer. The contrast is exciting! In the Old Testament, countless lambs were sacrificed as sin offerings. In the New Testament, in your temple lives the Lamb of God who takes away the sin of the world! In the Old Testament, the Temple furniture included a table of showbread and a golden lamp stand. In the New Testament, the One who declared, "I am the Bread of Life and the Light of the World" resides in you! During the old covenant period, the bright and radiant glory of God would appear in the temple on rare occasions. In this new covenant era, you can experience the manifested presence, power, and glory of the Spirit of God anytime and anywhere! All you have to do is offer up a sacrifice of praise. When the praises go up, the glory comes down! Heaven comes down, and glory fills your soul!

## God Assumes Ownership of Your Body and Spirit

God paid the highest price for our redemption—the death of His Son on a cruel cross. The ruby-red blood that flowed from His pierced body is the only acceptable currency to pay sin's price, for "without shedding of blood there is no remission," or forgiveness, of our sins (Heb. 9:22). The apostle Peter affirms, "Knowing that you were not redeemed with corruptible things, like silver or gold . . . but with the precious blood of Christ, as of a lamb without blemish and without spot" (1 Peter 1:18-19). His sacrifice makes Him owner of both your *body* and your *spirit*.

I wonder how many people come to Christ to be saved and get up from the altar thinking God has made claim to their spirit alone. Paul clears this up when he writes, "For you were bought at a price; therefore glorify God in your body and in your spirit, which are God's" (1 Cor. 6:20). When the Spirit of Jesus comes in to your body and unites with your spirit, He does not come as a guest. He comes as the owner of the house! He paid the mortgage and possesses the deed. He has the keys to the front door, and His room is the master bedroom. Consequently, He expects you to take care of His house, to keep it clean and free from sin, and to use it to bring Him glory, giving testimony to a lost world.

Unfortunately, the idea that "God owns my body" may be a hard pill to swallow for some. This is because, in America, we are consumed with our bodies and conquered by our appetites. We spend vast amounts of money to style our hair, whiten and straighten our teeth, lose weight, tone muscle, and lift up certain parts of our body that have begun to sag! Yet, we cannot or will not control our appetites. Instead, we give in to the desires of our flesh. One particular area is our sexual appetite. Advertisers use sex to sell everything from deodorant to hamburgers. Hollywood regularly portrays illicit sex in movies and on TV shows. Far too many Americans are unrestrained relative to their sexual appetite. The evidence is in the rampant adultery in many communities; in the number of people living together and having babies out of wedlock; and in society's belief that every teen needs a condom for safe sex because "they're going to do it anyway."

The culture in first-century Corinth is not unlike modern American culture. The people living in Corinth were incredibly liberal. Greek culture had influenced many to believe that the body was designed for immediate satisfaction of its desires and appetites. If you were hungry, you ate as much as you wanted and what you wanted. If you were aroused, you gratified the passion in any way you desired. The believers at Corinth were Pentecostal believers trying to impact the darkness with the light of God's truth. However, a problem developed: Some church members embraced the worldly, sinful culture in the name of "Christian liberty." I've run into this same thing as a twenty-first-century pastor. Church people say things like . . .

- "I can get drunk."
- "I can watch pornography."
- "I can have sex outside of marriage."
- "I can divorce my spouse and marry another person whom I *really* love."
- "I can be a glutton."

The danger in failing to recognize God's ownership of your body and spirit is that you may compartmentalize what you do with your body. You may develop a theology that says, "What I do with my body has no direct bearing on my spiritual life or my relationship with Jesus." Having made your body an independent dynamic, you will do things with it that are sinful and displeasing to the Master of the house.

Several years ago, a prominent pastor was the night evangelist at our denominational state camp meeting. Each night, he preached, prayed for people, and even spoke in tongues. Later, it became public that he was having an affair with another pastor's wife across town. How could a man of God step behind a sacred pulpit and minister to thousands each night knowing that he was living in sin? Somehow, in his mind, he was able to separate what he did physically with what he did spiritually.

You may be wondering, *How could God use a man like that as a camp-meeting speaker?* I used to wonder the same thing until I heard Dr. Ken Bell, one of my Bible college professors, give the best answer I have ever heard. He said, "What God does through a man is not necessarily a commentary on the man." In other words, any good the backslidden preacher did that week was a commentary on God, not on him. Clearly, the Lord was not pleased at all with his sinful ways. The Bible assures me the Holy Spirit was convicting him of his sin and urging him to repent. When his sin was finally exposed publicly, God mercifully gave him a chance to come clean once and for all. God does not separate what you do with your body from your spiritual life. He must be Lord of both your body and your spirit.

Whether or not an individual can drink alcohol and be a Christian is a popular topic lately. I have pastored members who drank socially, and I know ministers who drink alcoholic beverages regularly. For the record, I do not drink alcohol. My abstinence is based on Paul's writings in 1 Corinthians 6.

First, not everything is "helpful," or beneficial (v. 12), and I see no advantage in drinking. It does not help me in serving the Lord, and it does not help my testimony for Him. I had a son who drank heavily in high school and college, and I experienced firsthand how alcohol can devastate a family.

Second, I refuse to be "brought under the power" of alcohol (v. 12). Honest drinkers will confess they like the way the drink makes them feel. They like losing control, but I do not. If I am going to surrender myself, I want it to be under the influence of the Holy Spirit.

Third, I do not drink because my body is "the temple of the Holy Spirit" (v. 19). I do not know of one member in my church that would bring in an open bottle of beer or hard liquor into our sanctuary at any time. If we will not do it in the physical church building, how much more should we keep it out of the temple of our body, where the Holy Spirit dwells?

## Amazing Truth

I am amazed that the Spirit of God would take up residence in me! This thought overwhelms and encourages me. Because I have the Holy Spirit inside of me, I am assured continually that God knows me thoroughly. He knows what I am thinking and what I am feeling. No matter how good I am at hiding my thoughts or emotions from others, I can never hide them from the Lord. He knows the good, the bad, and the ugly in my life, which liberates me to be transparent and vulnerable before Him. If I sin, He knows immediately and responds with conviction. If I live righteously, He knows it, too. Because the Holy Spirit is always with me, He is completely aware of all I say and do. When I attend church, give my tithes, help someone in need, or suffer for my faith, God knows and rewards me!

Because of His Spirit within you, you are never separated from the presence of God. You may experience a crisis and feel like God has forsaken you, but emotions are deceptive. When Jesus was hanging on the cross, He felt forsaken by God. He cried out, "My God, my God, why have You forsaken Me?" (Mark 15:34). I have heard so many preachers and songwriters declare that God turned His back on Jesus while He was hanging on the cross, but it is not true. It is false theology. Jesus was quoting the first verse from Psalm 22, which was a messianic psalm written by David. The preachers and writers failed to read on to verse 24: "For He has not despised nor abhorred the affliction of the afflicted; nor has He hidden His face from Him; but when He cried to Him, He heard."

The Father never turned His face away from Jesus. He had His eyes on His Son all the time. This is important. If God turned His back on Jesus in His most critical hour, what stops Him from turning His back on you in your worst crisis? It is not going to happen. You may *feel* like God is a million miles away, but that does not change the *fact* that He offers "mercy" and "grace" in your "time of need" (Heb. 4:16). In your darkest midnight—in life's bleakest moments when your world comes crashing down and there seems to be no hope—God's Spirit is there inside of you! He is the Spirit of Truth who will "abide with you forever" (John 14:16). Because He is the Spirit of Jesus, He will "never leave you nor forsake you" (Heb. 13:5).

Adopt and pursue the following goals:

- Strive each day to keep the activities of your body and your spirit free from sin.

- Refuse to say or do anything that would set a poor moral example to your children or to a new believer in Christ.

- Avoid those things that potentially could bring you under their control.

- When tempted, remember that the Holy Spirit is right there with you, watching your every move. Do you really want to commit that sin in front of Him?

- Determine once and for all that how you live, in public and in private, is going to bring glory or recognition to God daily.

- Accept the fact that God's Spirit is always with you and allow that truth to give you faith when you don't feel God's presence.

# How Can You Be So Sure?

HAVE YOU EVER HAD ONE OF THOSE DAYS when nothing went right? When something or someone you were relying on failed you? The story is told of a young man who joined the Army and was assigned to the airborne division. He did not like the idea of jumping from a plane, but he had no choice. He went through paratrooper training, and the day arrived when he would make his first jump. The sergeant reviewed the basics: "When you jump, count to ten. Reach over with your right hand and pull your left cord on your main chute. If your main chute fails to deploy, reach over with your left hand and pull the cord on your reserve chute. When you land, a truck will be waiting to pick you up."

When the plane reached the proper altitude and position, the sergeant started sending soldiers out the plane's door.

When it was the young man's turn, the sarge had to push him out the door. He pulled his main chute cord and nothing happened. He pulled his emergency cord and nothing happened. As he whistled by, another soldier heard him say, "Yep, and I bet that truck won't be down there either."

Have you ever had days when you didn't feel saved? Have you ever had doubts about whether or not you will get in the pearly gates when you die or when the Rapture occurs? Two questions often asked by believers are (1) "How can I be sure I am saved?" and (2) "How can I be sure I am going to heaven?" The answer to both of these questions is found in the person of the Holy Spirit. His constant and continuing presence within the child of God guarantees salvation now and glorification in the future.

## How Can I Be Sure I Am Saved?

In Ephesians 1:13 and 2 Corinthians 1:22, Paul notes that every born-again believer has been *sealed* with the Holy Spirit. In ancient times, property and documents were sealed using hot wax and a signet. A *signet* was a stone or a ring with an engraving depressed below the surface, and the engraving represented the owner or his family. When pressed into the hot wax, it would make an impression that would match the engraving on the signet. The *seal* produced by the signet served to (1) identify *ownership*, (2) identify *authority*, (3) indicate *responsibility*, and (4) provide *security*.

If you have been saved, you have been sealed with the Holy Spirit. This "sealing" ensures you are under divine ownership and authority, God has assumed responsibility for you, and you are secure in Him.

*Ownership.* In the previous section, we learned that, when you are born again, the Holy Spirit takes up residence in your body and God assumes ownership of your body and spirit. He dwells in you twenty-four hours a day as the owner and master of the house. His presence in you is proof you are God's possession. You do not belong to the devil anymore, and the world and sin cannot rightfully lay claim to your soul. You are God's property! If He possesses you, you are saved, and you can rest assured you are right with God.

*Authority.* Being under God's authority is best described through an episode in the Easter story. When Jesus died and was buried in Joseph's tomb, He was placed in what was essentially a cave, with a heavy stone rolled over the entrance. The next day, the Pharisees and chief priests approached Pilate, the Roman governor who had crucified Jesus, and asked that the tomb be made secure by Rome. They feared that Jesus' disciples would come at night and steal away His body, giving the appearance that He had risen from the dead. Pilate gave them a detachment of Roman soldiers who sealed the stone door with the seal of Rome. The seal said, "This tomb is now under the authority of the Roman Empire. If you try to break this seal and open this grave, you will face the power and might of Caesar and the entire Roman Empire."

The spiritual correlation is awesome! Since I have been sealed with the Spirit, God sits on the throne of my heart, and I live to do His will. He is my Sovereign, and I serve Him as my Lord and King. The Holy Spirit's presence in me means I am now under the control of God. He is in charge of every aspect of my life. When anyone tries to come against me, God says, "Oh no! If you want to get to him, you have to go through Me!" As a subject and ambassador of the King of kings, I am covered by His sovereignty and protection. Living under God's authority gives me the confidence that my salvation and eternal destiny are secure in Him.

*Responsibility.* Paul maintains, "Therefore, my beloved . . . work out your own salvation with fear and trembling; for it is God who works in you both to will and to do for His good pleasure" (Phil. 2:12-13). Each believer is responsible for his or her spiritual life ("work out your own salvation with fear and trembling"). Unfortunately, in recent years we have seen many pastors de-emphasize personal responsibility and exaggerate the role of the local church. The line of reasoning goes something like this: "If you attend church regularly and volunteer for a ministry within the local church, you will automatically grow spiritually."

This has been the paradigm of many seeker-sensitive churches that have grown to mega-church status. Willow Creek Community Church near Chicago led the way in this approach. A few years ago, however, they admitted the model does not work. Pastor Bill Hybels said his people had become too dependent on the church for their spiritual growth and were expecting the church to feed them. The realization was that the more mature a believer becomes, the more they should take responsibility for their own spiritual growth. In response, Willow started coaching people to become self-feeders, creating a customized spiritual growth plan for every individual in their church. I applaud Willow Creek Church for making such a radical paradigm shift, and I continually encourage my members to take personal responsibility for their spiritual lives. This includes practicing the personal disciplines of prayer, Bible reading, fasting, and meditation on the Word.

So, is the success of your spiritual life dependent on your efforts alone? Absolutely not! Paul stresses that God himself is working on your behalf to help you fulfill His will. This is why the Holy Spirit comes to live inside you at the moment of your salvation. As you do your part, He is doing His part. Never think that God saved you and said to you, "Good luck! From this point on, you are on your own. I'll see you when you get to heaven!" He is working always with you for the completion of your salvation. The price He paid for your salvation was the greatest—the death of Jesus—and He is committed to do everything in His power to see you through all the way to glory! Consequently, you can rest peacefully each night knowing that God is determined to help you live right and make it to heaven.

*Security.* No one can snatch you from the Father's hand, and no one can take away your salvation. No one can remove the Holy Spirit from inside of you. No false teacher, false doctrine, cult, or devil has the power to separate you from the Spirit of the living God who dwells in your body and is joined with your spirit.

I live in the southern United States, where many people have been taught a doctrine often referred to as "unconditional eternal security." It argues that at the moment of your salvation, you are saved once and for all, no matter what. I do not believe in this doctrine. I do believe in what you might call "conditional eternal security." I believe that, as long as you meet the conditions laid out by God in His Word, you are eternally secure. That means keeping sin out of your life and keeping the Spirit of Jesus in you. It means continuing in the faith steadfast and grounded, refusing to be moved away from the hope of the gospel. The only person who can stop you from meeting God's conditions is *you*. The only one who can remove you from the Father's hand is *you*. As long as you remain in Him, you are secure in your salvation. Regardless of the persecution you suffer, the temptations you face, and the trials you endure, you are secure. The devil may whisper in your ear, "You're not saved," but that cannot change the fact you are secure in Jesus. You may not feel saved, but that doesn't alter the reality that you are right with God.

If you go to the post office to send registered mail, they will seal the envelope carefully. They will stamp it several times across the edges of the seal to be able to detect any tampering. If an unauthorized person tries to break that seal, they will face a serious penalty. Legitimately, only two people can open that envelope: the sender and the recipient. Similarly, God has placed within you the gift of eternal life, and He has sealed it within you by the presence of His Holy Spirit. God is the sender, and you are the recipient of His gift. God won't break the seal! You can break the seal if you backslide, but God will never arbitrarily withdraw His gift of salvation from you. A salvation prayer is not your assurance; the ever-abiding presence of the Spirit is your security.

## How Can I Be Sure I Am Going to Heaven?

In Ephesians 1:13-14 and 2 Corinthians 1:22, Paul describes the Spirit within as a *guarantee*. This word is a business term that speaks of earnest money, which is a part of the purchase price paid in advance as a down payment. It is the first installment, which guarantees full possession when the entire amount is paid later. Suppose you are house-shopping, and you find the house you want. You give the seller a certain amount (say $500 or $1,000) as *earnest* money. Once the seller takes the check, both the purchaser and the seller are pledged to complete the transaction. The earnest money serves as a guarantee that the house will be sold to you and to you alone.

One day, God found you and decided He wanted you for His own. He saved you from your sins, and He placed His Spirit in you as a down payment. He did this as a guarantee to you that He would return one day and complete the transaction! Jesus said, "In My Father's house are many mansions; if it were not so, I would have told you. I go to prepare a place for you. And if I go and prepare a place for you, I will come again and receive you to Myself; that where I am, there you may be also" (John 14:2-3).

How can you know for certain that Jesus will return one day for you? How can you be absolutely sure that heaven is your final destination and your eternal reward? The answer is exciting! Because He has deposited His Spirit in you, you can know with certainty that the Lord is pledged to closing the deal. He is committed to taking full possession of you when you die or when the Rapture occurs.

Have you ever put an item on layaway? You go to the layaway counter and make one payment, fully intending to get the article when you get the rest of the money. Your purchase sits in the store, but it is protected from other purchasers. As far as the store is concerned, the item belongs to you. What if you put a new, state-of-the-art TV on layaway, and what if the TV could talk? It would say to the other TVs, "I'm not like the rest of you TVs. I've been redeemed. I have a *sold* sign, and you don't. I may be in this store, but I'm not of this store. I belong to a new owner. I'm destined for his house, and he's coming for me any day now. I can't wait for my new owner to come and get me!"

In a sense, every born-again believer has been put on layaway. We are redeemed by the blood of the Lamb, and a first payment has been made by the deposit of the Holy Spirit in us. As far as God is concerned, we belong to Him now. Even the world knows we are not like them anymore, since there is something about us that indicates we are not what we used to be! We *are* different, because our status has changed. We are still *in* this world, but we are not *of* this world. Any day now, Jesus is coming back to get us, and He is going to take us to His Father's house. How do we know? The first installment has been paid—the Holy Spirit lives in us—and we should be saying every day, "I can't wait for Jesus to come and get me! Even so, come quickly, Lord Jesus!"

Ask yourself, "Am I sure I am saved? Am I certain I am going to heaven?" If you can answer "yes" to both questions, *rejoice*! If you cannot answer "yes," read Ephesians 1:13-14 and 2 Corinthians 1:21-22 right now. Next, state aloud the truths contained in these verses: "God owns me. I am His property. I am under His authority, and He has taken responsibility for my spiritual life. He is committed to getting me to heaven, and no one or nothing can stop that from happening but me. The Holy Spirit in me is all the assurance I need that I am saved and heaven is my reward!" Finally, thank the Holy Spirit for living inside you and for His continuing work in your life.

# PAPA GOD

IT IS SAD THAT SLAVERY has been part of the human experience for millennia, and human trafficking is a real problem still in many parts of the world. If you have never been a slave, you cannot understand what it is like to be in bondage to another human being. While you may read about it in a history book, you have no experiential knowledge of that kind of slavery. There is a spiritual form of slavery, however, that everyone is familiar with, and Paul addresses it in Galatians 4:1-7 and Romans 8:15-17.

## Those Whom the Son Sets Free

In Galatians 4, Paul acknowledges that, before an individual is born again, he is in bondage under two specific masters: (1) the elements of this world and (2) the law of God. The *elements of this world* are the basic principles or rudiments of the world—what I call the "ABC's of worldliness." They include false religions, humanistic philosophies, and warped moral systems embraced by individuals and cultures. Ultimately, those in bondage to the elements of this world commit sin. They think it is OK to cheat on your spouse if you don't love them anymore; it is acceptable to tell a lie in order to get out of trouble; and you should shift blame to someone else when you are accused of doing something wrong.

The *law of God* refers to the Ten Commandments. God's law has three fundamental purposes. First, it defines and outlines sin and righteousness ("Thou shalt" and "Thou shalt not"). Second, it serves as a standard of righteousness or morality—it defines and outlines how we are to live in order to please God. Third, the Law prepares sinful people for salvation through Christ by making them conscious of their sinfulness and their need of a Savior. Basically, the Law says to the sinner, "You need to be saved, and I can't save you. But I know the One who can—Jesus!"

Before Jesus provided salvation through His atoning work on the cross, God's perfect law enslaved people because they were asked to do the impossible—to obey the law of God perfectly. No one except Jesus Christ has ever kept all the Ten Commandments perfectly. In Matthew 19:16-22, we read of a rich young ruler who foolishly tries to convince Jesus that he has kept all the Law. Jesus quickly shows him that he has broken the first commandment because he has made a god out of his riches. Everyone has broken all the Ten Commandments. If you have not broken the letter of the Law, you have violated the spirit of the Law in some way. Even today, individuals who are not born again try in vain to keep the Law in some form or fashion, resulting in empty religions and empty religious experiences.

## The Great Emancipator

Jesus came to free us from the bondage of the elements of this world and the Law. In Galatians 4:4, Paul declares, "When the fullness of the time had come, God sent forth His Son."

Jesus came to redeem those who are under the bondage of the overseers of the world and of sin. Through His death on the cross, Jesus paid the price to free us from sin's slavery. Now, God adopts each redeemed slave as His son or daughter! Once we are born again, we are no longer slaves to sin and to the world's way of doing things. We are children of God and heirs of God through Jesus Christ.

Also, Jesus came to redeem those who are under the bondage of the Law. Jesus takes the religious woman and makes her a saved woman in order to free her from her futile attempts at keeping the Ten Commandments in her own strength. With His presence within her, she is empowered to do what she could not do before—to keep the Ten Commandments in letter and in spirit.

## Exactly What Do I Do?

God sent forth His Son into the *world* to *provide* salvation, but He has sent forth the Spirit of His Son into your *heart* to *assist you* in your salvation! Suppose all you have ever known is worldly, sinful living or empty religion. Now that you are born again, you may wonder, *I'm a son and not a slave anymore, so how am I supposed to act now that I am saved? How do I approach God?* Once again, the answer is found in the person and work of the Holy Spirit in you.

At salvation, God sends His Spirit—the Spirit of Jesus—into your heart, and He comes crying out, "Abba, Father!" (Gal. 4:6). *Abba* is an intimate Aramaic diminutive for "father." Jesus used "Abba" to address God the Father in the Garden of Gethsemane (Mark 14:36). Its equivalent in modern American

English would be "da-da or "pa-pa." When my boys were little, my wife, Leah, and I would compete with each other. She wanted their first words to be "ma-ma," and I wanted their first words to be "da-da." *Abba* is a tender term of endearment between a baby and his or her father. So, from the moment you are saved, the Spirit is saying to God the Father, "Da-da"—or, as I like to say, "Papa God!"

Why would the Holy Spirit do this? All you have ever known is sin and sinful living. You are clueless on how to relate to your new heavenly Father. Consequently, it is vital that the Holy Spirit teach you immediately how to be a child of God by modeling *intimacy*. Before salvation, you were distant from God. The Bible uses terms like "estranged" (Gal. 5:4) and "enmity with God" (James 4:4). Once you are saved, you have immediate access to God and are placed in a state of intimacy with Him. It is the kind of intimacy that a baby has with his or her parent. The Spirit teaches you to draw close to the Father and call Him "Papa God."

Singer and songwriter Nancy Harmon was the first person I heard refer to the Lord as "Papa God." I was a teenager, and I had never heard anyone to refer to God like that before. For a moment, I thought she had blasphemed! All my life, I had been taught that you referred to God as "our Father." I had heard people begin their prayers like this: "Our most gracious heavenly Father." Usually, it was a man with a deep voice, and the rest of his prayer was in Elizabethan English (King James style). Nancy had discovered the wonderful balance between the fear of the Lord and intimacy with the Lord. She knew Him reverently as Father but approached Him intimately as Papa God. That revelation changed the way I approached

God, and sometimes I call Him "Papa God" while in prayer. I have learned that, like a child, I can figuratively crawl up onto His lap and share my heart with Him, and He holds me in His arms and tenderly meets my every need.

## Transitioning From a Slave to a Child of God

As a slave, you lived in fear of God the Father because of the sin inside you. The Spirit of Jesus works in you to change your mind-set from that of a slave to that of a child of God! His role is to help you make the transition from *slave* to *son* in words, thoughts, and actions. He starts with your tongue and with your heart by teaching you that you can call to God and know He is hearing you. God the Father knows the sound of His Spirit's voice, but He knows the sound of your voice, too!

When I was nine years old, I was sitting on a large dirt pile about seventy-five yards away from our house. I was hitting a scrap board with a hammer, and I accidently sheared off a piece of wood and drove it into the side of my hand. I let out a blood-curdling scream! Even though I was at a distance from the house and Mom was inside with the doors closed, she heard my cry and came running to me immediately. My earthly mom knew the sound of her son's voice, and your heavenly Father knows the sound of your voice! The new believer must learn that God hears you when you are in pain, brokenhearted, worried, in distress, or in prayer. "The eyes of the Lord are on the righteous, and His ears are open to their cry" (Ps. 34:15).

In Romans 8:15, Paul refers to a "spirit of bondage . . . to fear." When you are an unredeemed slave, you are spiritually bound by a spirit of fear. Unregenerate people may say they do not believe in God or in divine retribution. Yet deep down, they fear the possibility that they may be mistaken and have to give an account to God one day for their life on earth. Some fear that life is a meaningless existence, where you are born, you live, you die, and you are done. Many fear (correctly) that their religious attempts are inadequate to make them right with God.

When you are born again, the Holy Spirit frees you from the bondage of fear. When He comes in, the fear leaves! First John 4:18 says, "There is no fear in love; but perfect love casts out fear, because fear involves torment." You no longer fear the judgment of God, dying and going to hell, or living a meaningless life. Second Timothy 1:7 says, "For God has not given us a spirit of fear, but of power and of love and of a sound mind." Sin gives you a spirit of fear, but God gives you the Spirit of Jesus to replace fear with assurance. He persuades you that Jesus took the punishment for your sins and loves you unconditionally. He provides you with confidence that you can live right and you are on your way to heaven. The Holy Spirit's presence and ministry in you verifies that your life has purpose and meaning.

My parents had only my sister and me, but my great-grandparents had fourteen children! In big families, one of the children may feel less loved or left out and become insecure. A discerning parent will talk with that child, getting them to open up about their worry or fear, and lovingly reassure the son or daughter that they are loved unconditionally. They will wrap arms of love around them and let them feel the warmth of their embrace. They will say, "I love you as much as I love all your brothers and sisters. You are special, and I'm so glad God gave you to me!"

Spiritually, we are in a big family. Sometimes, you might feel unloved or left out. It is not that God does not love you or that He has left you; it is because you feel this way. It is a false feeling. This can happen when you sin and repent. God has forgiven you, but you have not really forgiven yourself. You browbeat yourself, and that evolves into a feeling of insecurity. The devil will tell you that you are a second-rate child, and that God loves others in the family of God more than He loves you.

If you have ever had a season when you felt like you were in a spiritual wilderness, you have probably battled these feelings. You cannot feel the presence of God. While everyone else is shouting, singing, and rejoicing at church, you are standing there feeling numb. When Jesus was in the wilderness (Luke 4:1-13), Satan showed up to tempt Him. His tactic was to get Jesus to question His identity and His relationship with the Father: "If You are the Son of God. . . ." He still does the same thing to those in a spiritually dry season. He will say, "If you were still God's child, you would feel something. God must have rejected you." Thankfully, it is in those times that the Holy Spirit speaks softly to reassure you that you are still a loved child of God!

## The Language of the Father

It is natural and normal for children to learn the language of their father. Children with a Spanish-speaking father will learn to speak Spanish. Children with a German-speaking father will learn to speak German. Children with a Southern

United States father will learn to say, "Y'all" and "I reckon!" When I taught my boys to speak, I taught them to speak English. I started with "da-da" and "ma-ma." Eventually, I taught them to say other words in English, and their proficiency in their native language developed as they matured. They learned the meaning of multisyllable words and how to use those words in speaking and writing. In high school, one son learned French and the other learned Spanish. However, it all started when I gave them their first words to say.

As for the children of God, it is normal and natural to learn and to speak the language of their heavenly Father. The Holy Spirit begins by teaching you to say, "Abba, Father." As you read the Bible, He teaches you how to pray the simple promises of God. As you grow in the Lord, you become proficient in speaking the words of God in prayer, in your circumstances, and to others as a testimony. You comprehend deep truths and are able to articulate sound doctrine.

There is a time when God wants to fill you with His Spirit, which includes speaking in a language that is distinct from your natural tongue. It is a heavenly language, one that Paul references in 1 Corinthians 13:1: "Though I speak with the tongues of men and of angels. . . ." While I will deal more with this topic later in the book, understand that God wants to do so much in you. He wants to speak through you and work in your life in a powerful way, and it all begins with those first words: "Abba, Father."

# BAPTIZED INTO THE BODY OF CHRIST

THE HUMAN BODY IS A LIVING ORGANISM that has many members. A healthy body has hands, feet, arms, legs, eyes, ears, fingers, and toes. Each member is different, yet each makes a specific contribution to the entire body. The body, as a whole, contains a common life force that operates in every member.

The church of Jesus Christ is comparable to the human body. It has many different members, but together the individual members form one body. Each member makes a specific contribution to the church. Furthermore, the church has a common spiritual life or vitality that exists in all believers, and that force is the life of Jesus realized through the person and work of the Holy Spirit.

If you are born again, you are a member of the body of Jesus Christ. Local churches or fellowships contain members of Christ's body. However, they also have people attending who are not members of Christ's body because they have not been born again. You can be a member of a local church without being a member of the true Church (the body of Christ). Ideally, you should be a faithful member of a local church *and* a faithful member of the universal church of Jesus Christ.

## Placed Into Christ's Body at the Moment of Salvation

In any baptism, there are three components: (1) a baptizer, (2) a candidate for baptism, and (3) an element in which one is baptized. In 1 Corinthians 12:13, Paul testifies, "For by one

Spirit we were all baptized into one body—whether Jews or Greeks, whether slaves or free—and have all been made to drink into one Spirit."

This is one of those Bible verses that is often misinterpreted, so close examination is necessary. Paul is not talking about water baptism, but about salvation. First, the Holy Spirit is the baptizer; He is the One who is doing the baptizing ("by one Spirit"). Second, Paul's readers constitute the candidates for this baptism. There were people in Corinth who had put their faith in Christ. Paul even included himself in the identification of the candidates ("we were all baptized"). Third, the body of Jesus is the element in which the believers were baptized ("into one body").

Water baptism follows and symbolizes salvation. In water baptism, there is a baptizer, which is usually a preacher or pastor; there is a candidate for baptism, which is a new believer; and there is an element to be baptized in, which is a body of water.

There are two implications in baptism. First, baptism implies *identification*. Once, we had a church picnic at a state park situated on Lake Hartwell. We had some new converts who needed to be water-baptized, so we decided to baptize them in the lake during the picnic. I waded into the lake up to my waist, waiting for the first candidate. Soon, I felt something biting my legs. I could not figure out what was going on until I looked down in the water and saw a school of bream nibbling on my calves! That was the fastest water baptism I ever performed! As soon as each candidate stepped into the water, I quickly baptized them. It is impossible to be water-baptized unless you get in the water. Without exception, every person I baptized that day was *in* Lake Hartwell. Suppose I was baptizing Bill, and Bill's wife asked one of my church elders, "Where is my husband?" The elder would reply, "He's in the lake." In a sense, the moment each candidate stepped into the water, they immediately identified with the lake.

When the Holy Spirit baptizes you into the body of Jesus, you are immediately identified with Jesus. Without exception, every person who is born again is placed *in* Christ. In 2 Corinthians 5:17, Paul declares, "Therefore, if anyone is in Christ, he is a new creation; old things have passed away; behold, all things have become new." The phrase "in Christ" is Paul's most characteristic expression of what it means to be a true Christian. When you are saved, you identify with Christ by faith. You are identified as one who is in Christ, who belongs to Christ, and who serves Christ.

Second, baptism implies *union*. When water-baptized, a candidate is united with the water. In essence, he or she becomes one with the water. When the Spirit of God baptizes you into the body of Christ, He causes you to be joined with Christ and with those who comprise His body. In Galatians 3:26-28, Paul writes: "For you are all sons of God through faith in Christ Jesus. For as many of you as were baptized into Christ have put on Christ. There is neither Jew nor Greek, there is neither slave nor free, there is neither male nor female; for you are all one in Christ Jesus."

When you are baptized into Jesus, you put on Jesus. You are made to be one with Him through the union of your spirit with the Spirit of Jesus. You are also united with everyone else who has been united with Christ through Spirit-baptism.

Consequently, distinctions of race, rank, and gender are removed. The blood of Jesus and the work of the Holy Spirit make us one.

In the universal church of Jesus, our differences are wide and varied, ranging from skin pigmentation to cultural norms. Whether you travel across town or across the globe, you will see differences in the way believers talk, dress, and conduct worship services. Yet, these things are irrelevant to those who are in Christ. It breaks the heart of God when churches experience a lack of unity, difficulty in obtaining unity, or apathy in maintaining unity. Often, this occurs due to distractions by *secondary things*, such as denominations, cultural and social differences, the customs of their brand of religion, and racial preferences. Unity in the body of Christ and in the local church thrives when we stay focused on the *primary things*—a love for Jesus and a love for others.

It is vital that secondary things be dealt with and that each believer strives for the unity of the Spirit and the bond of peace. For too long, the world has watched in amusement and amazement as Pentecostals and non-Pentecostals have sparred with one another. What we share in common far outweighs our differences. It is time to lay aside our differences, find common ground, and strive for unity in the body of Jesus Christ! The gospel of Jesus Christ transcends the distinctions and differences that the world, sin, society, and culture have established. It levels the playing field with a call that says, "Whosoever will may come!"

There is not one Spirit that places the Pentecostals in the Pentecostal church and another Spirit that places the Baptists in the Baptist church. There is not one Holy Spirit that positions Presbyterians in the Presbyterian church and another Holy Spirit that sets people in the Methodist church. Denominations are man-made, and they can serve a good purpose. Instead, there is *one* Spirit, and He puts every believer into one church—the church of Jesus Christ! This concept alone should motivate us to tear down denominational walls and begin building bridges. If we did, it would result in instant camaraderie, connection, and fellowship in the body of Christ.

## Made to Drink Into One Spirit

According to Paul, the Holy Spirit places you into the body of Christ, and Jesus places the Holy Spirit in your body. He illustrates this by saying we "have all been made to drink into one Spirit" (1 Cor. 12:13). When you drink a beverage, the liquid leaves the cup or glass and flows inside of you. Likewise, when you are saved, the Spirit of God comes from Jesus and goes inside of you. When you are saved, you are drinking! Jesus makes you drink the Spirit because you have never tasted of the things of God before. In Psalm 23:2, the Good Shepherd *makes* the sheep "lie down in green pastures." Sometimes, God has to make us do things that are good for us. Aren't you glad He made you drink the Holy Spirit?

As a result, all born-again believers have the same Holy Spirit inside of them. If you are a redeemed child of God, the Holy Spirit in me is not a different Holy Spirit than the One in you. He is one and the same. Because you have the Holy Spirit and I have the same Holy Spirit, you and I are united as one. Consequently, you can often sense the Spirit of God in a people you do not know. This happened to Leah and me when we were in Jamaica for our twenty-fifth wedding anniversary. We were relaxing on the beach, and a young couple sat next to us. Because they were so close, I overheard their conversation, and something about them convinced me they were born-again Christians. Eventually, I struck up a conversation with them and discovered they were newlyweds from Nova Scotia. Finally, I asked them if they were spiritual people, and the young wife immediately replied, "Oh, yes! We are Christians!" I told them, "I knew it!" The Holy Spirit in them bore witness with the Holy Spirit in me that they were my brother and sister in the Lord!

Drinking of the one Spirit of God has profound effects in the body of Christ. A sinner who is born again on Sunday morning at a local church is quickly integrated into that fellowship because his spirit bears witness with the spirit of every member. He instantly becomes family! A family moves to another city and visits a church. In no time, they are acclimated and involved because the Spirit of God helps them to feel at home.

I have experienced the effects of drinking of one Spirit when I have gone on mission trips to Honduras. At the local churches, I am a foreigner—a *gringo*—and I stick out like a sore thumb. I am not dressed like everybody else, and I am taller than the rest of the congregation. I cannot sing the worship choruses or comprehend what the preacher is saying because I do not speak Spanish fluently. Yet, I feel quite at home in those churches. I feel the manifested presence of God during the worship services, and I feel a kinship with the people. I shake hands and hug necks with strangers, and we act like we have known each other our whole lives. Cultural differences are displaced by the reality of the Holy Spirit in us. Potential exclusion and seclusion are replaced with inclusion and acceptance as the Spirit removes all barriers and reminds us we are one in Jesus!

John 7:37-39 says, "On the last day, that great day of the feast, Jesus stood and cried out, saying, 'If anyone thirsts, let him come to Me and drink. He who believes in Me, as the Scripture has said, out of his heart will flow rivers of living water.' But this He spoke concerning the Spirit, whom those believing in Him would receive; for the Holy Spirit was not yet given, because Jesus was not yet glorified." This passage refers to drinking of Christ for salvation. It is an invitation to come to Jesus and drink, and now we understand that the person who accepts the invitation will drink of the Holy Spirit. If he accepts Christ, he will receive the Spirit of Jesus.

Jesus says, "Whoever drinks of the water that I shall give him will never thirst. But the water that I shall give him will become in him a fountain of water springing up into everlasting life" (4:14). When you are saved and drink in the Holy Spirit, it results in an internal spiritual fountain. It is as if you have a spiritual well inside that is fed by a never-ending spring. Just as a well serves as a water source for a residence, the Holy Spirit is given to you at salvation to help you become like Jesus. He produces the fruit of the Spirit, convicts you when you sin, and teaches you the truths of God. When you read the Bible, He helps you to grasp spiritual truths. When you worship, He makes certain you are doing so in spirit and in truth.

This first drink of the Spirit, however, should make you want more. Jesus promises that the drink, which becomes a well, can become rivers of living water within you! The rivers contrast with the fountain, illustrating the difference between receiving the Holy Spirit at salvation and receiving the fullness of the Spirit. While a well serves a home, rivers serve the populace, supplying cities and large geographical areas with water. Although I will deal with this topic later in the book, I want you to know that God wants you to experience more of His Spirit. He wants to fill you to overflowing, where He can use you to share His presence, His power, and His gospel to those in your community and around the world.

# Section II
## Living in the Spirit

# THE LAW OF THE SPIRIT OF LIFE

A WOMAN WHO WAS RECENTLY SAVED told her pastor, "I am so glad I am born again! Now, I will never have to battle sin or face another temptation! Praise the Lord!" Her pastor had to quickly inform her that, as much as he would love for that to be true for her, it was not the truth.

### Two Laws

Being born-again does not mean you will never have to deal with sin. Every believer will have to battle the temptation to sin until the day they die or until Jesus comes. Trust me on this one. I have been serving the Lord for over forty years, and I still have to overcome desires that are not of God. Even the apostle Paul admitted he was not immune from this spiritual struggle that is the norm for every child of God.

In Romans 7, Paul explains the internal warfare that plagues all humanity. He says there are two laws, or systems of operation, at work in me. First, there is "the law of my mind" (v. 23), which Paul also refers to as "the law of God" (v. 22). This is my understanding of right and wrong based on what I have learned from the Ten Commandments and from the moral precepts of the New Testament. The law of my mind is comprised of the things I know are right and that I ought to do. For example, I know I should not use God's name in vain or covet someone else's possessions.

Second, there is the "law in my members" (v. 23), or what Paul also calls "the law of sin and death" (8:2). It describes the weakness of my flesh in keeping God's moral law. Further, it describes the propensity of my flesh to commit sin, which is the opposite of God's moral law. Although I am born-again and have been made new in Jesus, I live in a body that has a depraved human nature and is antagonistic with the new nature I have in Christ.

Inevitably, this leads to a conflict between the law of my mind and the law of my members. My mind loves God's moral law and knows what it ought to do. My flesh, however, wants to do its own thing and rebel against what I know is right. Sometimes, my mouth wants to say what it should not say, my eyes want to look at something they should not watch, and my ears want to listen to something they should not hear. It is like the classic cartoon image of the devil on one shoulder and an angel on the other—except it is the law of my mind and the law of my members that are perched on my shoulders and screaming for my attention.

## The Third Law Makes the Difference

Thankfully, Paul reveals a third law or system of operation that gives you victory over your flesh, temptations, and sin. It is "the law of the Spirit of life" (Rom. 8:2). When you were born again, the Holy Spirit took up residence within you. Because He dwells within, He is constantly available to help you overcome your flesh nature with its evil desires, to obey God's moral law and do what is right. The law of the Spirit of life does not rule out the possibility of sinning, but it gives you the power not to sin. It does not make you immune to temptations, but it does give you the power to find the way of escape each time.

If you live in a state of conflict every day, refusing to live by the law of the Spirit of life, there are four negative results you can expect. First, you will experience *captivity*. Even though you know better, you will keep giving in to your flesh. Consequently, you will be bound by certain sins and by your sinful nature because you are allowing them to control you.

Second, you may live in a state of *confusion*. Some believers develop a wrong, fatalistic theology that says, "I keep trying and failing, so I'll just give in to temptation and sin and hope for the best." A few will go so far as to convince themselves they are still good Christians and right with God, in spite of their ongoing sinful decisions. However, God has made it clear in His Word that you can never rightly justify disobeying Him and His Word!

Third, you will know *condemnation*. If you know God's law and still give in to your flesh and sin, both your conscience and the Holy Spirit will convict you. If you develop a lifestyle of sin, where you are habitually giving in to temptation and practicing sin, you will backslide and be under the judgment of God. If you keep sinning and repenting, over and over, you will beat up on yourself constantly, living with self-condemnation.

Fourth, you will reach a place of *concession*. The devil will tell you, "You can't live for Jesus!" The world will say, "Stop this religious foolishness and come back to us!" Tired of the fight, you will eventually give in and quit. After trying and failing multiple times, you will throw in the spiritual towel because you feel your flesh is too strong.

Here is the wonderful news: You do not have to sin! You can say no to temptations and yes to God. You do not have to be carnal because the Holy Spirit frees you from the law of sin. When you were saved, you crucified your flesh, rendering it powerless. When the Roman soldiers crucified Jesus, His hands and feet were nailed to the cross, and He could not move. He could speak, but He was immobilized. I want you to imagine your sinful nature nailed to a cross. It can scream for satisfaction, but it can do absolutely nothing to get its way. Because it is nailed to the cross, it has no power or influence over you. You can make right choices when you stand at the crossroads of a moral decision because your flesh is powerless and the Holy Spirit in you is powerful!

## Which Way Are You Going to Walk?

In Romans 8:1, Paul mentions two types of lifestyles—walking "according to the flesh" and walking "according to the Spirit." When you walk according to your flesh, you give in to the desires of your carnal nature, and you live to gratify the lusts of your body. It is more than being sensual or giving in to sexual lusts. It means you live on an earthly, material level, divorced from any significant contact with the Spirit.

When you walk according to the Spirit, you give in to the desires of the Holy Spirit. Rather than listening to your flesh, you listen to the Spirit of God and live in a way that is pleasing to Him in everything. It is living at a spiritual level, where you see things from God's perspective. Your mind and heart are set on heavenly, spiritual matters. When this occurs, you do not *have* to go to church; you *want* to go to church! You want to read and obey the Bible, and you long to pray and worship the Lord. Your heart's desire is to be filled with the Spirit and to be like Jesus in character. You want to witness, work in God's kingdom in some capacity, learn spiritual truths, and grow in the Lord.

In Romans 8:4, Paul speaks of those who are *walking in the Spirit*, and in verse 5 he speaks of those who "*live according to the Spirit*." A literal translation of this last phrase is "those who are of the Spirit." Paul uses the Greek participle *ontes*, from which we get our English words *ontology* and *ontological*. *Ontology* is a philosophy that deals with the nature of being or existence, so verse 5 is an ontological statement. What does that mean? *Walking and living in the Spirit is not just something you do—it's who you are!* It is the essence of your being, and it is why you exist. If I should ask any born-again believer, "Why are you here? Why do you exist?" the correct answer would be, "To walk and to live in the Spirit!" Being born-again and living in the Spirit gives you the *what* and the *why*, providing spiritual *pursuits* (prayer, Bible reading, witnessing, etc.) with a spiritual *purpose* (spiritual living).

Once you see that living in the Spirit is the reason for your existence, your entire perspective will change. Spiritual activities that were once boring and perfunctory will come alive! You will pray to experience communion and intimacy with Jesus, and you will read your Bible to hear from the Lord. People, events, and goals that once seemed so important will take a backseat to your foremost desire to fulfill His purposes for your life. How you live in private, when no one is around, will be consistent with how you live in public, because you always live to please God.

Walking and living in the Spirit always results in a radically different lifestyle from the life of sin. You walk and live in the Spirit each day and all day long—not just on Sunday. You act and speak righteously when something good happens to you (like getting a raise) or when something bad occurs to you (like getting passed over for a promotion). Whether you are in a room with other believers at a church event or eating dinner at a restaurant with unregenerate people on a business trip, you please the Lord. If you are with a carnal Christian who morally compromises because of his surroundings, you stay the course and remain true to Christ. Why? Because living in the Spirit is not something you *do*—it is who you *are* regardless of whom you are with or your circumstances.

## Every Day, You Have a Choice to Make

Suppose that this morning, when you arose from bed, you determined to live in the Spirit. You went through the whole day and overcame sin and temptation, and you feel pretty good right now. You made it. You enjoyed God's presence and power in your life, and you can go to sleep tonight knowing that you fulfilled your God-given purpose. Tomorrow, however, you will have to start all over.

Each day, you have to make a decision. On one hand, you can be carnally minded, leaning toward the things of your flesh and being a "carnal Christian." If that is your choice, you will struggle to live for Jesus and will grieve the Holy Spirit. Instead of being sold-out and fully obeying God's Word, you will look for loopholes so you can gratify your flesh and still be "saved." You will fail miserably, because you cannot please God at all when you are carnal and are walking according to your flesh. Fleshly living will kill everything relative to the Holy Spirit. It will choke the life from your relationship with God, the spiritual life within you, your relationships with other believers, and your witness.

On the other hand, you can choose to be spiritually minded, inclining toward the things of God. A decision to live according to the Spirit means you will enjoy life and know wonderful peace. You will live the victorious Christian life and be a healthy, growing Christian. Your relationship with God and other believers will be vibrant and strong. There will be no discrepancies in your witness, and you can go to bed each night knowing that you lived the day to please Him.

In Romans 8:12-13, Paul exclaims, "Therefore, brethren, we are debtors—not to the flesh, to live according to the flesh. For if you live according to the flesh you will die; but if by the Spirit you put to death the deeds of the body, you will live." I know a couple facts about debtors. First, debtors have financial obligations. They are obligated to pay their debts until they have paid back everything they borrowed. Second, those in debt are obligated to their lenders. Proverbs 22:7 states, "The rich rules over the poor, and the borrower is servant to the lender." In a sense, the person or institution that lends you money has power over you.

Because you have been born again and have God's Spirit inside you, you are not obligated to your flesh. If you are struggling to serve God because you keep leaning toward carnal things, stop living like you owe your flesh something! You are obligated to the Holy Spirit, and you owe Him everything! He convicted you and showed you your need of a Savior. He gave you new birth and implanted a new nature in you. He cries out, "Abba, Father" and teaches you intimacy with "Papa God." It is the Holy Spirit who patiently bears with you, who placed you in the body of Christ, who lives in you and loves you. He pours out God's love in your heart and makes the presence and power of Jesus real in you. His presence overwhelms you when you are in an anointed atmosphere! He comforts you when everyone else has deserted you. Stop catering to your flesh and begin catering to the voice of the Spirit of God. Tell your flesh to leave you alone, to back off. Inform your flesh that the affair is over! There is a new love in your life, and you owe Him everything!

## Are You Walking and Living in the Spirit?

How would you describe your spiritual life? Are you guilty of catering to your flesh too much, at the neglect of spiritual matters? Are you yielding to what the Spirit of God desires in every area of your life? Are you walking in the Spirit in how you treat your spouse, children, friends and coworkers? Are you living for Jesus consistently or are you a chameleon, changing moral colors depending on whom you are with at the time?

I know these are tough questions, but it is important that you answer them honestly if you want to be certain you are walking in the Spirit. If you can honestly say that living in the Spirit is not what you do or who you are, I challenge you to put down this book and have a little talk with Jesus! Confess your sin and carnality and ask the Holy Spirit to begin working in you in a transformative way. He will give you the strength and the resolve to put to death immoral thoughts, words, and actions. He will help you make right choices and please your Papa God in every way.

# LED BY THE SPIRIT

IN HIS BOOK *Surprised by the Voice of God*, Jack Deere tells the story of one of his seminary students, named Robert. Jack was his Hebrew professor, and Robert had come to his office to ask for mercy for a late assignment. In the course of their conversation, Jack was deeply impressed by the Holy Spirit that Robert was struggling with pornography. By all outward appearances, Robert was the model Christian, but Jack could not ignore the leading of the Spirit. Finally, he asked Robert if he was into pornography, and the student ashamedly admitted that he had struggled with the sin since he was a young teenager. After confession and prayer, he left Jack's office for-given and hopeful.

## A Spirit-Led Lifestyle

If you are walking according to the Spirit, the Holy Spirit will lead you. In Romans 8:14, Paul reveals, "For as many as are led by the Spirit of God, these are sons of God." *Being led by the Spirit* is more than a synonym for being a Christian. Rather, it is a determining factor of whether or not you are a child of God. Just as a child knows the voice of his natural father and obeys, the born-again believer knows the voice of the heavenly Father through the Holy Spirit and obeys His Word at all times. The Greek word translated "led" in this verse is a present partici-ple, noting ongoing action. This verse could be translated accu-rately, "For as many as are *continually being led* by the Spirit of God, these are sons of God." Submission and obedience to the promptings of the Spirit is a lifestyle for the believer.

To be *led by the Spirit* means to be "carried along by the Spirit" in the sense that He is guiding you. Certainly you are accustomed to many people giving you directions. Your spouse, parents, boss, teacher, financial adviser, and doctor are just some of the people who tell you where to go or what to do in order to be successful. You exercise some level of trust in order for these people to be permitted to speak into your life. Likewise, the Holy Spirit guides you so you can avoid failure and experience victory in your walk with God. This means you must be confident in His ability to lead you in every area of your life. To be led by the Spirit is a *faith* issue. The Bible repeatedly says, "The just shall live by faith" (Rom. 1:17; Gal. 3:11; Heb. 10:38).

For the Spirit of God to be your guide, you must answer yes to these questions: "Do I trust Him? Am I willing to submit to His will? Am I convinced that He knows better than I do and that He is looking out for my good?"

## Grieving the Spirit of God

One of the most foolish things you can do is ignore the leading of the Holy Spirit. If you do, you will grieve Him. In Ephesians 4:30, Paul warns, "Do not grieve the Holy Spirit of God, by whom you were sealed for the day of redemption." Any time you reject the Holy Spirit's guidance, He feels sorrow and pain over your disobedience. I believe His sorrow is manifested as a deep disappointment in your refusal to trust and obey.

Let's face it: How often have we frustrated God by our unwillingness to do things His way? This reminds me of an incident that occurred between my dad and my maternal grandfather when I was a teenager. My grandfather was building a house so he could retire from pastoring, and my dad and I were spending a lot of time helping him. My dad is an excellent and experienced finish carpenter. One day, Dad and my grandfather were doing some finishing work, and Dad was trying to show Pappaw a better and quicker way to do something. Pappaw was stubborn and refused to listen to Dad, insisting on doing things his way (which happened to be a slower and less efficient way). My dad got so frustrated that I could almost see steam boiling from under his collar. The whole thing was very entertaining to me!

As Christians, I wonder how many times we are guilty of stubbornly insisting on doing things our way. We frustrate the

Spirit of God—who knows a better way—and we inevitably suffer the consequences of our poor choices.

## Lead Me Not . . .

I have found only one place in the Bible where we are instructed to ask God to *not* lead us—the Lord's Prayer. Jesus instructs us to pray this way: "Do not lead us into temptation, but deliver us from the evil one" (Matt. 6:13). The word *temptation* can mean "to entice to evil" or "to try or put to the test." Because we know God does not tempt a person to sin or lead a person to commit a sin, the second meaning must apply here.

In John 16:33, Jesus makes a promise I do not like very much: "In the world you will have tribulation." Because I live in a fallen and sinful world, potentially I can face pressures, problems, and perplexities daily. If it was not for the grace of God, experiencing trials, tests, and trouble might very well be the norm every day of my life. In this same verse, however, Jesus makes another promise: "But be of good cheer, I have overcome the world." Through prayer, God will lead me away from potential trials, steering me clear of the difficulties this world is ready to dish out!

It is only fair to warn you that God may answer no to your prayer. Occasionally, God takes His children through difficult circumstances in order to try their character and faith. A good example of this is Job. He was a righteous man, but Satan wanted to disprove his faithfulness to the Lord. God chose to lead Job into the most trying experiences of his life, knowing that His servant would remain faithful through every trial he faced. God, however, had something else in mind. Job's response to his tragedies revealed that he was somewhat self-righteous, and God used the difficulties to purge Job. He did not go through his trial because he was a *bad* man; he went through it to make him a *better* man.

When things go miserably bad in my life, the first question out of my mouth is normally, "Why is this happening to me?" Perhaps the better question to ask is, "Lord, why are You leading me into this trial?"

I believe there are two major reasons why God would lead me through trying times. First, He might be attempting to show me a weakness in my character. If I am self-righteous, proud, or bitter, God will not ignore these heart issues. He might use a trial to reveal these sins and show me my need to repent.

Second, it could be He wants to produce certain traits in me so I can be more Christlike. For example, one of the fruits of the Spirit is *long-suffering,* or "patient endurance." It is the ability to endure persecution and ill-treatment, and it describes a person who has the power to exercise *revenge* but uses *restraint* instead. Now think about this: I cannot develop or reflect this trait unless I am persecuted or mistreated! I am learning that if God leads me into a trial, it is for my greater good.

## Where He Leads Me I Will Follow

The Holy Spirit will lead you in many ways, but I believe the area in which we desperately require His guidance is in making *moral decisions.* Although you may be walking according to the Spirit, it is possible for you to falter for a moment and give in to the sinful desires of your flesh. Of course, this

WHEN THE NATURAL MEETS THE SUPERNATURAL

is never the will of God for you. So, when your flesh rises and demands gratification, the Holy Spirit will speak and lead you to put to death any sinful deeds. Your goal is to listen to Him rather than your flesh. When you do, you will make a right moral decision. The more you are led by the Spirit and put to death immoral acts, words, and attitudes, the more you will be like Jesus and be conformed to God's holy standard.

The fictional town of Mayberry, North Carolina—where the main character, Andy Taylor, is sheriff and Barney Fife is his deputy—is the setting of *The Andy Griffith Show.* In one of my favorite episodes, Andy's son, Opie, and some other boys get into mischief, including breaking a street lamp. Barney goes on a tirade about their behavior, compelling Andy to point out they are only eight-year-old boys. Barney replies, "Yeah, well, today's eight-year-olds are tomorrow's teenagers. I say this calls for action and now. Nip it in the bud! First sign of youngsters goin' wrong, you got to nip it in the bud!"

While many people may think the phrase "nip it in the bud" originated with Barney Fife, it is actually a horticultural term. Sometimes, a plant produces buds that will render the plant unhealthy or inhibit growth and production. The gardener or farmer recognizes this and removes the bad bud. Even though it is part of the plant, it does not belong and has to go.

Likewise, the Holy Spirit knows when your flesh desires to sin. If you satisfy your wicked desire, the resulting sin will make you spiritually unhealthy, inhibit your spiritual growth, and stand between you and God. So, the Holy Spirit will say to you, "Don't consider this sin; it doesn't belong in your life. Refuse to give in to it. Nip it in the bud now!" If you will listen to Him and follow His lead, you will nip that sin in the bud by making a right moral choice and walk in purity and holiness.

## The Voice Behind You

Isaiah 30:21 is a beautiful Old Testament promise with powerful New Testament relevance. The prophet declares, "Your ears shall hear a word behind you, saying, 'This is the way, walk in it,' whenever you turn to the right hand or whenever you turn to the left." The voice behind you is the voice of the Holy Spirit. If you choose to listen to His voice, you will walk in the Spirit and in obedience to God.

But what if you listen to the flesh and take initial steps in a morally wrong direction? When you move from following the Spirit to walking away from the Spirit, He is no longer in front of you. You have moved off the path of righteousness, putting Him behind you. Yet, in incomprehensible love and grace, He calls out to you: "You're going the wrong way! Stop! This is the way—this is the right choice to make—this is what God wants you to do! Repent and follow Me once again."

You should realize that some moral decisions are easier to make than others. Often, the tough ones are reflections of the sinful proclivities of your life before salvation. Consequently, you may be tempted to downplay the importance of total obedience and settle for "doing the best you can" or simply make excuses for your sin. Whatever you do, never give in to these temptations because too much is at stake. God is Lord of your life, and you must please Him rather than pleasing your flesh. The Holy Spirit's goal is to help you do that.

In Psalm 23:3, David says of the Good Shepherd, "He leads me in the paths of righteousness for His name's sake." Your obedience to the Spirit's leading is vital because how you live is not only a reflection of you; it is also a reflection of Jesus! I have two sons who obviously share my last name. When they both lived at home, I taught them how to make right moral choices. When they failed to do what was right, it was a bad reflection on them and a poor representation of our family name. My dad said something powerful to me once, and I made sure to pass it along to my sons: "Don't say or do anything that would bring a reproach on God, your family, or the church." The only way to avoid any reproach is by depending on the power of the Holy Spirit within and by following His voice.

### "I'm Watching Your Life"

It was the beginning of a new school year, and a teenage boy sat in his first-period class. A new girl sat in the desk behind him, and eventually they broke the ice and spoke to each other. As the weeks went by, they talked more and more about their lives and personal interests. Eventually, the topic of religion came up, and the young man told the girl that he was a Christian. She responded that she was a Christian also and she could tell he was one from the first day they met. She said, "I make it a point to find a teenage Christian to watch and to be a spiritual role model for me. In my last school, the person I chose let me down."

The young man answered, "That's too bad. Who are you watching now?"

She calmly replied, "You!"

People know if you are a child of God, and they are watching to see if what you profess matches up with how you live. The Holy Spirit is committed to leading you in making wise moral decisions for the sake of your testimony and for the glory of God.

Take personal inventory and see how well you are doing as a follower of the Spirit. Have you learned to listen to His voice? Do you trust Him enough to do what He says? Is there an area of your life where your wrong choice continually grieves the Holy Spirit? Are you willing to repent and submit to His leadership? Are you "nipping in the bud" those desires of your flesh that keep getting in the way of doing God's will? Through prayer, address any issues with God and ask Him to open your ears to hear what the Spirit has to say!

# THE WAR WITHIN

THROUGH HIS APOSTOLIC AUTHORITY and by the inspiration of the Holy Spirit, Paul issued many commands in his letters. One example is in Galatians 5:16: "Walk in the Spirit, and you shall not fulfill the lust of the flesh." When you obey this command, you are living your life in the power of the Spirit—being led by the Spirit, listening to Him, and pleasing Him in everything. You are living on a spiritual level, with your heart and mind set on the things of God. Now, do not misunderstand me: I am not talking about living a fanatical life. The church has seen far too many "granola-bar Christians"—the fruits, flakes, and nuts! I am talking about leading a normal life with normal activities but remaining occupied with the Holy Spirit and engaging in the things that matter the most to Him. Consequently, one year from now you will be further along spiritually than you are right now.

### "I Hate Flesh"

A member of my church admitted to me that she has a problem: she cannot stand to hear the word *flesh*. She says there is something about how the word sounds when it is pronounced that makes her cringe. Once, I preached a message that required me to say *flesh* multiple times. After the service, she told me my sermon almost drove her crazy. I suppose she would not like to hear me read what Paul pens after his command in verse 16: "For the flesh lusts against the Spirit, and the Spirit against the flesh; and these are contrary to one another, so that you do not do the things that you wish" (v. 17).

I do not hate the word *flesh*, but I do despise my flesh and the trouble it creates for me. This New Testament concept focuses on the carnal, inbred, inherent tendencies of my human nature. I have the treasure of salvation in a jar of clay called my "flesh" that is weak and has a propensity to do what is contrary to the law of God. It is a constant enemy of my soul that does not care at all about pleasing God. It cares about only the gratification of its wants and the satisfying of its desires, reflected in what Paul calls the "lust of the flesh." The word *lust* means "desire" or "passion," and in this case it refers to an *evil* desire or passion. It comes from the Greek word *thumos*, from which we get our English words *thermos* and *thermostat*. So, the lust of the flesh is a rise in temperature of unbridled passion, requiring some means to regulate the desire so sin is not committed.

I live in South Carolina, where it gets extremely hot and humid in the summer. However, I can deal with the heat, because I have an air-conditioning system in my home controlled by a thermostat. When the temperature rises outside and causes the temperature to rise inside, I cool off the house by adjusting the thermostat. By the push of a button, cool air flows through the ductwork into each room, and the house cools down. The thermostat regulates the temperature so the living conditions are enjoyable instead of unbearable.

When God saved you, He moved into your body, made it His home, and put in a "spiritual air conditioner" called the Holy Spirit. When the temperature of your flesh rises and wants to get sin in the house, the Holy Spirit steps in and helps you to regulate or control the desire of your flesh. As you listen to Him and lean on His power, you refuse to give in to the sinful desire. Your obedience keeps the living conditions of your heart pure and enjoyable for the presence of God. If you, instead, give in to the lust of your flesh and bring sin into your body, you create an environment that is unbearable for a holy God.

## Internal Warfare

Billy Graham once told the story of an Eskimo fisherman who came to town every Saturday afternoon. He always brought his two dogs with him—one was white, and the other was black. He had taught them to fight each other on command. Every Saturday afternoon in the town square, the people would gather, the two dogs would fight, and the fishermen would make bets. On one Saturday, the white dog would win, and on another Saturday, the black dog would win—but the owner of the dogs would always win his bets! His friends began to ask him how he did it—how did he know which dog would win the fight? He replied, "I starve the one and feed the other. The one I feed always wins because he is stronger" (*The Holy Spirit*).

This story describes the struggle between the flesh and the Holy Spirit. Your flesh desires to say or do one thing, and the Holy Spirit inside you wants you to say or do another. They are at war with each other, and this conflict is ongoing. In fact, this internal warfare will continue until death or until Jesus comes! In the war against terror, the United States government has made it clear time and again that it will not negotiate with terrorists. Similarly, the Holy Spirit will not negotiate with your flesh, and your flesh will not compromise with the Spirit. This is a battle to the death. The only way you can win is by starving the flesh to death by refusing to satisfy its sinful desires and by nurturing the things of the Spirit daily.

Oftentimes in an action movie, the hero will face the villain in a final showdown. The hero will say, "When this fight is over, one of us is going to walk away, and one of us isn't!" In the war within your body, the Holy Spirit is the hero, and your carnal flesh is the villain. While your flesh will never destroy the almighty Spirit of God, it does have the power to destroy your spiritual life. To guarantee victory, the Spirit wants you to kill the sinful lusts of your flesh. If you side with your flesh in a battle for right or wrong, you will kill the presence and the power of God in your life. If you put to death the flesh with its evil passions and desires, you will defeat carnality and win the fight for right.

If you do not learn how to walk in the Spirit, you will be of all Christians most miserable. You will know what you ought to do—what God wants you to do—and God will use that knowledge to convict you of your sins. You will ask Him to forgive you, intending to repent. The next time your flesh rises up, however, you will cave in again . . . and again . . . and again. You will fall into a vicious cycle, where you feel guilty all the time and live a defeated life.

This is not God's plan for you! Jesus did not suffer and die horribly for you to live a carnal and sinful life. His death was the ultimate blow to Satan and sin; He gave His life so you could win the victory over your carnal self. Do not settle for a defeated life. Instead, appropriate the power of the Cross to every temptation and lean on the power of the Spirit of Jesus to say no to your flesh and yes to God.

## A Strategy to Win

Perhaps you are wondering, *What can I do to overcome my flesh, learn to listen to the Holy Spirit, and live a life daily that will please the Lord?* Using military jargon, I want to give you a strategy to be a winner.

*Practice good reconnaissance.* Reconnaissance is an exploratory military survey of enemy territory. It is used to gather information necessary to win the battle. In the armed forces of the United States, often the Green Berets or Navy SEALs serve in this role. They slip behind enemy lines prior to the major battle to learn as much as possible of the enemy's strengths and weaknesses. The knowledge they relay back to headquarters gives troops information they need to defeat the opposing force. Also, Special Forces will disrupt or destroy the enemy's lines of communication to make it difficult for them to coordinate any attack.

To win the spiritual battle between your flesh and the Spirit, you must practice reconnaissance on *you*. Try to step back for a moment and take a good look at yourself. In what areas are you spiritually strong, and in what areas are you spiritually weak? What sins and temptations give you the most trouble? Make a list of the issues you struggle with the most.

Some sins are driven by carnal *nature* (your flesh), while other sins are driven by carnal *nurture* (nourishment). Are you watching something on the Internet that is feeding your desire to sin? Are you hanging out with a group of friends or dating someone who fosters sinful lusts? Are you listening to music or are you going to places that encourage you to satisfy the evil passions in your body? Like the Green Berets, you must recognize the sources of trouble and eliminate them.

In Matthew 18:8-9, Jesus warns, "If your hand or foot causes you to sin, cut it off and cast it from you. It is better for you to enter into life lame or maimed, rather than having two hands or two feet, to be cast into the everlasting fire. And if your eye causes you to sin, pluck it out and cast it from you. It is better for you to enter into life with one eye, rather than having two eyes, to be cast into hell fire." Jesus is not proposing self-mutilation! Instead, He is trying to make a radical point for His disciples: Do not tolerate anything or anyone in your life that will stand between you and God. Remove the negative people and influences, even if that means breaking up with that boyfriend or finding a new set of friends to hang out with on the weekend.

*Completely obey your superior officer's orders.* In his narrative poem, "The Charge of the Light Brigade," Alfred Lord Tennyson paints a graphic picture of a battle fought during the Crimean War in 1854. Describing the brave soldiers of the British Light Brigade, he writes: "Theirs not to make reply / Theirs not to reason why / Theirs but to do and die." Soldiers are not supposed to question their officers or the orders they give to their troops. They are instructed and trained to trust their officers and to fully carry out every command.

Victory over evil lusts and sins is possible if you will listen to and obey the voice of the Spirit. He knows the temptation you face and the way to defeat it. First Corinthians 10:13 says, "No temptation has overtaken you except such as is common to man; but God is faithful, who will not allow you to be tempted beyond what you are able, but with the temptation will also make the way of escape, that you may be able to bear it." God has a plan that will make you an overcomer, but you have to trust and obey. The hymn says, "Trust and obey, for there's no other way to be happy in Jesus, but to trust and obey."

Some sins are avoided through *divine prohibitions*. You know the moral law of God in your mind, and you possess a solid and Biblical standard of right and wrong. At the moment of temptation, you comply with God's precepts, resulting in obedience and right moral action. However, some sins are avoided by *divine inhibitions*. We have all had moments when we faced a moral challenge and were unclear regarding the right thing to do. At those times, the Holy Spirit brings His Word to your mind or issues a personal warning. In your spirit, you experience a definite prompting of the Spirit of God, telling you, "This is what you need to do." The inhibition is so certain that you know what you are sensing is from God and the right course of action.

*Show the enemy no mercy.* In 1836, General Antonio López de Santa Anna and the Mexican Army surrounded a small Catholic mission called the Alamo. Inside, a small group of defenders, led by Colonel William Travis, were determined to hold the mission at the cost of their lives. When the Mexican general sent a courier requesting surrender, Travis responded by firing one of the mission's cannons. Santa Anna laid siege for a week and a half, battering down the mission's walls. On the day of his final assault, he flew a red flag and played the "El Degüello" bugle, signaling that no quarter or mercy would be given to the defenders. In a vicious battle with hand-to-hand combat, the Mexican Army took the mission. Seven men tried to surrender, but they were summarily executed. Santa Anna had made it clear he would show mercy to no one.

Know that your flesh is a stubborn enemy, and it has no intention of surrendering. It wants to be free to do what it wants and when it wants, but you cannot afford to let that happen. It will fight you daily, and it will not give up until the day you die. You cannot afford to be considerate of your flesh and its desires. So, raise the red flag and make up your mind that you will not offer quarter to your flesh. Show your flesh no mercy! Refuse to give in to it and, by the Spirit, bring it into submission to the will of God.

*Use the weapons at your disposal.* The U.S. Army is successful at taking a civilian and turning him into a soldier. They will put several different weapons in his hands and teach him how to use them. When they are finished with him, he will be skilled in using those weapons to eliminate his enemy in war. The Army will issue him a rifle, and he will be prepared to fire his rifle at an enemy soldier across the battlefield without a second thought. He knows that his enemy has been trained, too. If the civilian-turned-soldier does not kill his enemy, his enemy will kill him.

You are a soldier fighting a spiritual battle against your flesh, and God has issued you spiritual weapons:

- *Prayer.* When your flesh is screaming for gratification, stop what you are doing and ask the Holy Spirit to help you do the right thing. Prayer will line you up with the will of God and help you avoid giving in to the flesh.

- *The Bible.* When you are at a moral fork in the road, go to God's Word for direction. It is a "living and powerful" weapon that will give you victory over sinful desires (Heb. 4:12).

- *The Church.* Godly members of your local church fellowship offer accountability, making it more difficult to give in to vile lusts. They also provide models of how to live the victorious Christian life.

## Never Give In!

In 1941, Great Britain was at war with Germany. Winston Churchill was the prime minister, and in October of that year, he gave an inspirational speech at his alma mater, Harrow

School. I have often heard that he said, "Never give up" in his speech, but this is not true. He said:

> Never give in. Never give in. Never, never, never, never— in nothing, great or small, large or petty—never give in, except to convictions of honor and good sense. Never yield to force. Never yield to the apparently overwhelming might of the enemy.

If you will listen, you will hear the voice of the Holy Spirit saying something similar to you:

> You are in a great conflict. An axis of evil—the devil, the world, and your flesh—is out to destroy your soul. Daily, you must fight for the right. Some days, you will feel weak and be tempted by your flesh to give in to corrupt passions. Sometimes, you will be defeated because you will yield to the desires of your flesh. The devil will tell you that you can't live for God, and the world will oppose your faith. You may be tempted to simply throw in the towel and turn your back on God. *Never give in!* Never, never, never, never—no matter how great or small the temptation may be for you. Never yield to your flesh. Give in to Me! I will give you the strength to win the war within you. Greater is He that is in you than he that is in the world!

How are you doing as it relates to the battle within? Are you walking in the Spirit or are you fulfilling the lusts of your flesh? Do some reconnaissance and make a list of the areas of your life where you struggle the most. Pray about these issues and discover what God's Word has to say about them. Cut off any negative sources that are nurturing sin in your flesh and ask a fellow believer to keep you accountable. Remember: God is living inside of you, and He is an ever-present help in your time of trouble. If you will call on Him, He will give you victory!

# THE FRUIT OF THE SPIRIT: BEING LIKE JESUS

THE BIG QUESTIONS OF THE AGES have always been: "Why am I here? What is my purpose in life?" Outside of Christianity, many believe that life has no purpose or meaning. They think you are born, you live your life, and you die. Some believe if there is any purpose in life, it will be self-determined or self-discovered. While that sounds good, it rarely plays out into anything substantive. Rather, it usually leads to a selfish life.

The born-again child of God who embraces the Bible as the source of all truth believes in an existential purpose. He believes that his life has a divinely mandated purpose—he exists for a reason. This divine purpose is found in Romans 8:29: "For whom [God] foreknew, He also predestined to be conformed to the image of His Son." In Galatians 1:15-16, Paul confesses his belief that the reason he was born—the reason for his existence—was so God could reveal His Son in him.

To put it simply, humans exist to be like Jesus. God created man in His own image, but Adam's sin in the Garden of Eden shattered the image. Jesus, however, came to save fallen humanity from sin and its tragic consequences and to restore the image of God. This restoration occurs by the presence and the power of the Holy Spirit in redeemed men and women. Up to this point in this book, I have listed several reasons why God placed His Spirit inside of you when you were born again. Now, I am giving you the number one reason why the third person of the Godhead dwells inside of you: He lives in your heart so He can cause you to *be like Jesus*.

An unfortunate myth in Christianity goes something like this: "If I do all the right things—if I read my Bible enough, pray enough, and attend church enough—I can be like Jesus." Praying, reading the Bible, and attending church are essential elements in one's spiritual formation, but it takes the Spirit of Jesus to transform a person into the image of God's Son. While the child of God does play a part in the process, it requires a work of God to become like God in character.

The Holy Spirit conforms you to the image of Jesus by producing the fruit of the Spirit in you. "The fruit of the Spirit is love, joy, peace, longsuffering, kindness, goodness, faithfulness, gentleness, self-control" (Gal. 5:22-23). In essence, they are the godly characteristics of Jesus. They are the attributes that serve as evidence that you are being conformed to the image of Christ. If I can see the fruit of the Spirit in you, I will see Jesus in you! Let's examine these nine traits.

## Love

Jesus outlines the two Great Commandments: "Love the Lord your God with all your heart, soul, and mind. Love your neighbor as you love yourself" (see Matt. 22:37-40). The Holy Spirit in you makes you a lover. You will love God, and you will love people. You will even love the people who are antagonistic toward you. I know that sounds crazy, but Jesus commands us to love our enemies (5:44). Years ago, I was in a worship service listening to the general overseer of the Church of God, Dr. Charles Conn. He was preaching on love, and he made a statement that rocked my world. He said, "God has called me to love people I don't even like!" How is that possible? Love is a choice, and by the Spirit's enablement, you can choose to love those who may not love or like you.

Being a pastor, I often visit my members when they are in the hospital. Sometimes, they are in the emergency room or in some other restricted area, and I need to get to them as quickly as possible in their medical crisis. To assist me, the hospital has issued me an identification badge. If someone from my church is rushed to the ER, I simply show my badge to the desk attendant, and I get instant access. Although I am not employed by the hospital, my badge identifies me with the rest of the medical personnel.

God's love manifested in and through you is a lot like my hospital badge. In John 13:35, Jesus declares, "By this all will know that you are My disciples, if you have love for one another." As you love your brothers and sisters in Christ selflessly, sacrificially, and unconditionally, you are immediately identified by the world as one who is an authentic child of God.

## Joy

*Joy* is an inner experience of elation that comes from being right with God. It is often contrasted with *happiness*, which comes from external influences. Joy flows from within. You can be in the middle of a trial or be persecuted for your faith and still know the joy of the Lord. Someone might ask you,

"Why do you smile so much? How can you maintain your excitement and positiveness, even when things aren't going well for you?" You can tell them, "I am full of joy because Jesus lives in me!"

People who possess the fruit of joy are people who rejoice. In Philippians 4:4, Paul challenges us, "Rejoice in the Lord always. Again I will say, rejoice!" The joy on the inside has to show up on the outside. Each Sunday at our church, the music is lively, the lyrics are inspirational, and the musicians and singers are anointed. The vast majority of the congregation is singing, clapping their hands, and smiling. Some are jumping up and down, rocking back and forth, or dancing before the Lord. Their praise and worship to God is how they rejoice in the Lord for all He has done for them. Occasionally, we sing a chorus that declares, "I gotta praise Him!"

## Peace

*Peace* is freedom from strife internally. It is the sure confidence that everything is going to be fine because God is in control. Because you are born again, you have peace *with* God. As a result, the Holy Spirit causes you to know the peace *of* God. He gives you peace that counteracts any negative emotions that try to create strongholds in your heart and mind.

Have you noticed how people are so stressed? Men and women are anxious and worried about their jobs, the economy, their children, their marriage, their health, and their finances. A little stress is normal for the average person, but living in a perpetual state of anxiety is not normal or healthy. In Philippians 4:6-7, we find the antidote for worry and stress:

Be anxious for nothing, but in everything by prayer and supplication, with thanksgiving, let your requests be made known to God; and the peace of God, which surpasses all understanding, will guard your hearts and minds through Christ Jesus.

Like a sentry at the gate of a military post, God's peace will prevail over every anxious thought and feeling and keep you at rest in your soul.

## Longsuffering

This fruit of the Spirit, *longsuffering*, is patient endurance, especially if you are bearing up under suffering or persecution. Jesus said, "In the world you will have tribulation" (John 16:33). The apostle James wrote, "My brethren, count it all joy when you fall into various trials, knowing that the testing of your faith produces patience" (James 1:2-3). Nowhere in God's Word are you promised a carefree and untroubled life. Even as a believer, you will experience some pressing and painful moments. My good friend, Pastor Steve Sylvie, says life is a contact sport, and sometimes bad things happen to God's people. Most of the hardships you face will be the result of living in a sinful world. The car will break down, the economy will have a negative effect on your finances, or your heath will deteriorate. Some of your trouble will occur because you are serving Jesus, and evil people will try to make your life difficult.

Let's be honest: Anyone can exhibit a strong faith in God in the good times. When we are on top of the world, we do not have a problem trusting God or encouraging a brother in Christ who is in a living hell. But what about those times when our world is rocked, or our crisis is so bad that we are at the end of our rope and hanging on desperately? I believe this is where the Bible stories of the heroes of faith come to our rescue. These men and women of God had enduring faith in famines, in fires, in the lion's den, and in jail. They never gave up on God, but they persevered in their faith in the worst of times.

This is what the Holy Spirit will help you to do. Perseverance in hardship manifests genuine faith, and He uses the trials of life to teach you how to trust God at all times. Better yet, your patient endurance is a testimony of the effectiveness of the power of Christ in you.

## Kindness

I have spent my whole life hanging around God's people, and the vast majority of them are good and godly. However, I have encountered a few who call themselves "Christians" who are ill-mannered, rough, hard, cruel, legalistic, and strict with people. Unfortunately, I am not the only person who has met them. Waitresses tell me the meanest customers they have are so-called Christians who come to their restaurants after church on Sunday. These servers share horror stories of how these "Christians" speak rudely to them, treat them like dirt, and tip poorly or not at all. Believers who possess and manifest the fruit of kindness are not mean to servers in restaurants.

In his book *Les Miserables*, Victor Hugo tells of Jean Valjean, whose only crime was a theft of a loaf of bread to feed his sister's starving children. He was arrested and served nineteen years as a convict. He was released and unable to find work, but he came to the house of a good bishop who kindly gave him supper and a bed for the night. Giving in to temptation, Jean stole the bishop's silver plates and slipped out, only to be caught by the police and returned. The bishop said, "Why, I gave them to him. Jean, you forgot to take the candlesticks."

Jean was overwhelmed by the bishop's act of kindness, wondering how the man of God could show him such mercy and compassion after he had stolen from him. At that moment, he repented and was saved from his sins.

God used the bishop's kindness to attract Jean to Jesus, and this is what the Holy Spirit will do through you. The fruit of *kindness* means you will smile and speak graciously to everyone, regardless of their status or station in life. You will be cordial and show genuine interest in those around you. You will be friendly, helpful, and considerate of the feelings of others. You will be merciful and forgive the person who wrongs you. You will exhibit a graciousness that attracts people to Jesus.

## Goodness

There is a twofold meaning to this word. It describes *doing* good and *being* good, addressing both conduct and character. Someone has said this fruit is love in action. Certainly, it implies generosity because good people who do good to others are ultimately givers.

In Matthew 5:16, Jesus proclaims, "Let your light so shine before men, that they may see your good works and glorify your Father in heaven." An act of benevolence from a righteous individual has the power to reflect the glory of God. The recipient sees beyond the giver and gets a glimpse of the God living in the giver. In a world where so many are stingy and cold, the Holy Spirit will use you to reveal the love and the grace of God to people who are in need of a revelation of Jesus.

## Faithfulness

*Faithfulness* is a prerequisite for stability and health. Banks lend money anticipating the faithfulness of the loan recipient to make monthly payments. Children anticipate the faithfulness of their parents in providing food, shelter, and clothing for them. Governments anticipate the faithfulness of foreign powers in maintaining treaties. In your spiritual life, the fruit of faithfulness is necessary for a stable and consistent Christlike life.

The result of this fruit is *dependability*. God's people are supposed to be trustworthy and reliable. For example, you should do what you say you are going to do—you should keep your word. God should be able to count on you to maintain your godly convictions at all times, not just when it is convenient. You should live right whether you are in public or in private, with no one around to watch you. Your goal should be to stand before God one day and hear Him say, "Well done, good and *faithful* servant."

## Gentleness

Perhaps a better word here is *meekness*. This is a disposition that is even-tempered and balanced in spirit. Meekness is not weakness, but it is power and strength under control. Jesus was meek, but He drove the money changers out of the Temple. When attacked by the Pharisees, He stood His ground, but He never used His divine power to harm them.

This fruit of the Holy Spirit is vital because it makes you genuine. It is the difference between being pretentious and unpretentious. I am sure you know a few pretentious people. They tell you how much they have accomplished in this life, the degrees they have earned, and the names of the powerful people they know. They exaggerate who they are and what they have done in order to impress you.

If you are gentle, you are unpretentious, and the only person you are interested in impressing is God the Father. You live to please the Spirit, which liberates you from worrying about what others think about you. He frees you to be a servant of Jesus, to speak the truth in love, or to confront a sinning brother or sister in Christ in humility and grace.

## Self-Control

*Self-control* is the ability to voluntarily abstain from anything that might hinder you spiritually or cause you to sin. It implies the restraint of all natural desires relative to thoughts, words, impulses, and actions. When Satan tempted Jesus in the wilderness to sin, the Lord showed incredible self-control. He refused to give in to the devil or the desires of His flesh. Instead, He chose to comply with the will and the Word of God.

Too much of a bad thing will hurt you, and too much of a good thing can do damage as well. Obviously, the Spirit

WHEN THE NATURAL MEETS THE SUPERNATURAL

of God is going to do all He can to keep you from yielding control to your flesh or to a temptation and committing a sin. However, He will also assist you in avoiding excesses that can do spiritual harm (like too much social media, work, and recreation). In Proverbs 16:32, Solomon warns, "He who is slow to anger is better than the mighty, and he who rules his spirit than he who takes a city."

We live in a time when the masses seem to have lost restraint. "If it feels good, do it" is the cry of the world. Drug problems are epidemic, alcoholism is mounting, and pornography and profanity are rampant. You cannot afford to get caught up or bound up by the things of your flesh or the corruption of this world. Jesus is depending on you to shine His light and to share His plan of salvation with those in spiritual darkness and captivity.

## You Get What You Sow

In the natural world, God has established a law of sowing and reaping. It is a simple law. If you have a garden, and you sow okra seeds, you will grow okra. If you sow squash seeds, you will eventually harvest squash. Paul was aware of this law and how it applies to your spiritual life. In Galatians 6:7-8, he cautions, "Do not be deceived, God is not mocked; for whatever a man sows, that he will also reap. For he who sows to his flesh will of the flesh reap corruption, but he who sows to the Spirit will of the Spirit reap everlasting life."

Daily, the Holy Spirit is sowing into your life, developing in you the characteristics of Jesus. Are you sowing to the Spirit? Are you investing your time, energy, attention, and money into the things of God? Jesus commands us to "seek first the kingdom of God and His righteousness" (Matt. 6:33). As the Holy Spirit does His part, you need to do your part. Over time, you will see gradual changes and realize you are becoming more and more like Jesus every day.

# Shining With His Glory

Ordinary people can reveal the extraordinary glory of God. Paul declares, "We all, with unveiled face, beholding as in a mirror the glory of the Lord, are being transformed into the same image from glory to glory, just as by the Spirit of the Lord" (2 Cor. 3:18).

If you are born again, you will shine with the glory of God through the reflection of the character of Jesus Christ. As a transformed child of God, the Holy Spirit is working in you and through you to shine Jesus to the people around you. People will look past your facial hair, eyeglasses, hairstyles, and clothes and see Jesus. They will look beyond your education, job title, and position in an organization and recognize Jesus inside of you. As you are working on a project, troubleshooting, or brainstorming with a team, someone will glance over at you and realize something about you is making them think about the Lord! Your goal is to cooperate with Him daily by refusing to walk in the flesh and choosing to walk in the Spirit. You never want to reflect a blurred or distorted image of Jesus.

If you have satellite service for your television, you have a satellite dish somewhere on your property. As long as the sky is clear and the weather is dry, you will get a nice, clear, high-definition picture on your TV. If a strong thunderstorm comes through, however, the heavy rain and the thick clouds may block the signal beaming down from the satellite. The picture on your TV screen will be distorted and may even disappear, and this message will appear: "Searching for a signal."

When you are living right and walking in the Spirit, you display a "high-definition" picture of Jesus in your life. When you decide to walk in the flesh, however, the heavy rain of sin distorts His image. Thankfully, the Holy Spirit within convicts you, and you search to reestablish a divine signal by quickly seeking for repentance and forgiveness. The spiritual signal is immediately restored, and the image of Jesus is clear to everyone watching your life.

## Glowing

I know of two men in the Bible who literally glowed with the glory of God, and one of them was Moses. For forty days, Moses had been in the presence of the Lord on Mount Sinai. When he returned to the camp of Israel carrying the Ten Commandments, the Israelites "were afraid to come near him" because his face was glowing supernaturally with the divine glory of God (Ex. 34:30). He had been in God's presence so much that His glory had rubbed off on him. When the people saw Moses, they looked beyond him and saw Divinity. At that moment, Moses reminded them more of God than he did of himself.

When you were saved, God came inside of you through the presence of the Holy Spirit and put a glow on your face. It was not a supernatural manifestation like Moses experienced, but it was real nonetheless. You probably had a new grin, and people at work or at home said, "What happened to you? There's something different about you!" They were noticing the glory of Jesus in you! You were different because old things had passed away and all things had become new (see 2 Cor. 5:17).

Back to Moses. The supernatural glow on his face made some Israelites uncomfortable. It was weird and abnormal to them, but Moses did not care what they thought. He liked having the glory of God resting on him. Eventually, he noticed the glow was fading, so he put a veil over his face. He did not do this because he did not want people to see him *with* God's glory; He did it because he did not want people to see him *without* God's glory (see Ex. 34:34-35; 2 Cor. 3:13)! As long as his face was shining, he kept his face uncovered. When the glory faded away, he put on the veil. Why? *He would rather be seen with the glory of God than without it.* He preferred to be known as one who shined with the glory of God.

Each day of my life, I have a decision to make: to cover up the manifestation of Jesus in me or let Jesus shine through me for all to see. Honestly, I prefer that people see me *with* His glory than see me *without* it. I know living like Jesus seems abnormal to the world and may shake up a few unbelievers, but those things do not deter me. I want desperately to be known as one who reflects the glory of Jesus.

If you are a newborn in Jesus, you are a changed man or woman. Some of your family and friends will be supportive, but others will not like the new you. They may tease you and attack you for your faith, saying you are weird and your faith makes them uncomfortable. You will be tempted to put a veil over the glory by giving in to the persecution and by reverting to your old, sinful ways. Do not do it! Let people say whatever they want to say about the change in you. Prefer to be known as someone who has been changed and saved! The Holy Spirit will shine Jesus through you to them, drawing them to Christ to be freed from their sin.

Moses faced some frustration because of the glory of God fading over time. To fix this, he would go into a place called the Tent of Meeting, where God would meet with him. I do not know if it took a few minutes or an hour, but spending time with God in intimacy and communion was adequate to restore the glow on Moses' countenance. Returning to the camp, he would eat, chat, judge, and lead with a glow on his face. When the glory faded again, he would return to the Tent of Meeting once more and spend time with God, and he would leave shining with God's glory. *He did what was necessary to be certain people never saw him without the glory.*

In this New Testament era, the glory of Jesus does not fade away, like it did for Moses. The ever-abiding presence of the Spirit means the glory of Jesus is shining in you twenty-four hours a day, seven days a week. Spending time with the Lord in intimate communion will intensify the manifestation of His glory! Second Corinthians 3:18 says the Spirit transforms you "from glory to glory." In other words, as you spend time with Jesus and serve the Lord, the glory of Jesus will increase in you! I have discovered that, as I spend time in prayer, praise, worship, and in the Word, I come out of those experiences with God a changed individual.

The only thing that can mar or cover the glory of Christ in you is sin. It is important that you keep sin out because disobedience to God will put a veil over His reflection in you. If you sin, you should remove the veil by confessing your wrongdoing and repenting. Keep short accounts with God so you are not guilty of having lingering, unconfessed sin standing between you and the Lord. Resist temptations and always look for the way of escape. Follow the Spirit's leading and make godly moral decisions. Do what is necessary to be sure the people in your life never see you without His glory. You never want to lose the glow!

## "One of Us Has Got to Go!"

My father-in-law's name is Jim Talley, and he understands what it means to shine with the glory of Jesus. He was born in Georgia, and he grew up in a highly dysfunctional home. His father was an alcoholic, and his irresponsibility and absence forced Jim to grow up fast and help his mother raise his three brothers. When he was a teenager, he secured a good job at a local store, and the money he earned helped meet the family's needs.

Everything was going great until Jim went to church and gave his life to Jesus. God placed His Spirit inside of him, and it was evident that he was born again. Soon after he was saved, his boss approached him and said, "Jim, I know what has happened to you. You have become a Christian. I can see it all over you. I once served the Lord, but I am backslidden. Since you were saved, I have felt conviction every time I get around you." What he said next floored my father-in-law: "I can't keep living under conviction, so one of us has got to go—and that means you. You are one of the best workers I have ever had, and I'll give you a great reference to anyone who calls me. I'm sorry, but you cannot work here anymore." Jim shined with the glory of Jesus so much that it cost him his job!

One of my favorite heroes of the faith is Smith Wigglesworth. Smith lived in England in the nineteenth century and at the turn of the twentieth century. He was a plumber who was saved and baptized with the Holy Spirit and fire. God gave him a powerful apostolic ministry whereby countless people were saved, delivered from the devil, and healed. God even used him to raise several people from the dead!

One day, Smith went into a store to purchase shoes. He said nothing to the clerk, but he noticed the man got fidgety. Smith ignored him and continued looking at shoes. Finally, the clerk came over and said, "Sir, who are you? Ever since you walked in, I feel the presence of God and am under heavy conviction for my sin. I cannot take it anymore! Who are you?" Smith told him who he was, and then he led the young man to salvation through Jesus.

At work, at home, in church, on the golf course, or while shopping in a shoe store, the Holy Spirit wants to manifest Jesus through you. As you crucify your flesh and put on the Lord Jesus, people will look past your humanity and see divinity. They will see beyond your flesh and recognize the Son of God in you.

## Release the Glory

The other person who glowed with glory in the Bible is none other than Jesus Christ. The Lord led Peter, James, and

John up on a high mountain, where He was transfigured before them, glowing with the glory of God (Mark 9:1-3). Moses and Elijah suddenly appeared talking with Jesus, and the three disciples were terrified (vv. 4, 6). Peter's reaction to that supernatural experience is laughable: he suggested that they go into a building program! "Rabbi, it is good for us to be here; and let us make three tabernacles: one for You, one for Moses, and one for Elijah" (v. 5).

What was Peter thinking? In his Jewish mind-set, the glory of God was supposed to be confined to a building. God the Father spoke from heaven and said, "This is My beloved Son. Hear Him!" (v. 7). I think God was saying to Peter, "Stop that nonsense! I'm not limiting My glory to a temple anymore. Because of My Son and the new covenant, I'm going to release My glory in the physical body of redeemed people!"

For whatever reason, Peter and the other apostles had difficulty seeing past the humanity of Christ. The Transfiguration was significant because they saw for themselves how the glory of God could shine through a human being. This was God's plan, and Jesus served as the prototype of what was to come. "And the Word became flesh and dwelt among us, and we beheld His glory, the glory as of the only begotten of the Father, full of grace and truth" (John 1:14).

As they descended the mountain, Jesus commanded Peter, James, and John not to tell anyone about what they had seen until after His resurrection. They obeyed, but I am not sure they understood why. They had not fully grasped the idea that Jesus was going to die a sacrificial death and rise from the dead. It was not until after the first Easter Sunday that they finally comprehended the command. After the Resurrection, every saved man and woman, indwelt by the Holy Spirit, would reflect the glory of the risen Savior!

## "I Can't Take Anymore!"

Moses and Jesus glowed, and the children of Israel and the disciples were terrified. Terror is never the proper response to a move of God, but far too many believers recoil in fear from sensational and supernatural revelations of God's glory. They are afraid because they are operating more in their flesh than they are in the Spirit.

Has the Holy Spirit ever tried to move on you in a supernatural way and you resisted Him? Be honest. Were you afraid of losing control, facing the unknown, or being embarrassed? If you want to experience the fullness of God's glory in and through you, it is critical that you learn to yield fully to the Spirit. When you do, wonderful things will happen in your spiritual life!

During a powerful South Carolina Church of God Camp Meeting, Darrel Croft and I were lying on the platform. We were associate pastors at the same church, and the night evangelist had just prayed for us. Because of the overwhelming power of God, we had fallen to the floor and were praying intensely. Darrell and I were in full view of two to three thousand people in the congregation, but we were oblivious to them. We were not afraid of what they were thinking because we were caught up in the glory of God's strong presence. We had been under the weight of God's glory for some time, and it was incredibly heavy. Suddenly, I heard Darrell say something that caught my ear. Before I tell you what he said, you have to know that Darrell is 6 feet 5 inches and weighs 285 pounds. He is an ex-college football player who turned down an offer to play in the NFL to preach the gospel. My big friend cried, "God, You've got to stop! I can't take anymore! I can't take anymore of Your glory!"

You may be thinking, *I want to manifest God's glory and reflect Jesus, but I don't want His manifested glory falling on me like that. I just don't see the need.* Let me give you the rest of the story. While lying on that platform floor, God spoke to Darrell and me about becoming church planters. Later, Darrell planted a church in Columbia, South Carolina, and I planted a church in Anderson. Our experience under God's glory was a reference point that sustained us as we faced the thrills and challenges of church planting.

## God Is Not Into Buildings

Did you begin this chapter thinking God's glory is confined to a church building? If so, it is time to embrace the truth. God is not into buildings anymore! Sure, church facilities are important for worship services and ministry, but God doesn't stay in the sanctuary after the doors are locked. He goes with you in the tabernacle of your body everywhere you go.

Acknowledge the work of the Holy Spirit in shining Jesus through you daily. As you go to work, school, or the department store, be aware that God wants you to be a reflection of His Son to your coworkers, friends, and store clerk. Pray, "God, transform me from glory to glory!"

# Section III
## The Power of the Spirit

# THERE'S MORE

JOHN THE BAPTIST was the forerunner of the Christ, and he cried out two great declarations of Jesus: (1) "Behold, the Lamb of God who takes away the sin of the world!" (John 1:29) and (2) "He will baptize you with the Holy Spirit and fire" (Matt. 3:11). What was John saying? *Everyone should have an encounter with Jesus as Savior, and everyone should have an encounter with Jesus as the Holy Spirit Baptizer.*

If you have been born again, the Holy Spirit is not foreign to you. He has been with you from the moment of your new birth. He took up residence inside of you as the Spirit of Jesus and as your Comforter. Your reception of Him at salvation was real, and He has been working in you every moment of every day. However, God's Word makes it clear that you can have

WHEN THE NATURAL MEETS THE SUPERNATURAL

more of the Spirit. You can realize a greater measure and dimension of Him than you know right now. It requires an experience separate from your new birth. What is it? The terminology from the Scriptures is fluid. It is called *being filled* with the Spirit, *receiving* the Spirit, or having the Holy Spirit *fall on*, *poured on*, or *come upon you*. Most often, this wonderful blessing is referred to as "the baptism with the Holy Spirit."

## What Is It?

When filled with the Spirit (baptized with the Holy Spirit), you become a recipient of divine power. In Acts 1:8, Jesus said to the apostles, "You shall receive power when the Holy Spirit has come upon you." He also told them, "Behold, I send the Promise of My Father upon you; but tarry in the city of Jerusalem until you are endued with power from on high" (Luke 24:49). The word *endued* means "clothed." Jesus promised to clothe Peter, James, John, and the other disciples with power straight from heaven! This promise is for all of God's people, which means God wants to clothe *you* with His supernatural power!

This experience of God's clothing us with spiritual power is for intensified service and witness for Jesus Christ. He gives us His power by His Spirit to enable us to do what Jesus did when He walked the earth. Everywhere He traveled He healed the sick, helped the hurting, and testified to the truth and the grace of God. Jesus was concerned that after His resurrection and ascension to heaven, His ministry to helpless, hurting, and sinful people would continue through His Church. He made the baptism with the Holy Spirit available so we could be effective in service for Him. He wants us to spread the

Gospel to everyone. He wants us to undo what the devil has done, loose what the devil has bound, heal what the devil has hurt, and mend what the devil has broken.

## The Two *Greats*

Just before returning to heaven, Jesus shared with His disciples the Great Commission and the Great Command. The Great Commission is found in Matthew 28:18-20:

> "All authority has been given to Me in heaven and on earth. Go therefore and make disciples of all the nations, baptizing them in the name of the Father and of the Son and of the Holy Spirit, teaching them to observe all things that I have commanded you; and lo, I am with you always, even to the end of the age."

The Great Command is located in Acts 1:4-8:

> Being assembled together with them, He commanded them not to depart from Jerusalem, but to wait for the Promise of the Father, "which," He said, "you have heard from Me; for John truly baptized with water, but you shall be baptized with the Holy Spirit not many days from now." Therefore, when they had come together, they asked Him, saying, "Lord, will You at this time restore the kingdom to Israel?" And He said to them, "It is not for you to know times or seasons which the Father has put in His own authority. But you shall receive power when the Holy Spirit has come upon you; and you shall be witnesses to Me in Jerusalem, and in all Judea and Samaria, and to the end of the earth."

The promise of Spirit-infilling was given by Jesus in the context of *evangelism*. The Great Commission said, "Go," but the Great Command said, "Wait." Jesus was saying to His followers, "Before you witness, wait; before you do any evangelistic work, wait; before you try to win the lost, wait. I don't want you to wing it; I want you to wait." Before they were to go preach the Gospel, they were required to wait and pray until they received the power of God to effectively proclaim the Good News. The disciples' obedience to the Great Command is recorded in the Book of Acts, which is the historical record of the Church. Chapters 1 and 2 are about the Church *waiting* for and receiving the outpouring of the Holy Spirit, and chapters 3 through 28 are about the Church *winning* the world for Christ.

The purpose of the baptism with the Holy Spirit is to equip and empower you to be a productive evangelist! You are commissioned to go and tell people that a man named Jesus died, rose again, and lives to save them from their sins and make them right with God. To a sinner, the facts of the Gospel can seem preposterous and absurd. To the natural man, the Incarnation and the Resurrection provoke cynicism, skepticism, doubts, and questions. God's answer is to show an unbelieving world that Jesus is real and very much alive . . . through you! The combination of a Christlike character and the manifestation of God's supernatural power in you will make you an effective witness.

## It's a Kingdom Thing

In Acts 1, the disciples were concerned about Jesus establishing a literal kingdom, where they would be ruling and reigning with Him. They were tempted by the desire to have political power. Jesus made it clear His kingdom was not about *ruling* people; it was about *reaching* people with the Gospel.

His kingdom would be comprised of Spirit-filled people with divine power who are passionate about reaching a lost and dying world.

If you are from a non-Pentecostal background, you have a doctrinal detour to avoid. Because the baptism with the Holy Spirit has been a major emphasis of Pentecostal churches, you may be tempted to write it off as a denominational thing. Nothing could be further from the truth. Acts 1:3 says Jesus spent His post-resurrection time with the disciples "speaking [about] the things pertaining to the kingdom of God." Being filled with the Spirit is not a *denominational* thing; it is a *Kingdom* thing. There are born-again and Spirit-filled Anglicans, Methodists, Baptists, Mennonites, and Catholics.

Doubters have come up with all kinds of alternate explanations for the baptism with the Holy Spirit. Some say you are filled with the Spirit when you are saved. It is true you receive the Holy Spirit at your new birth. However, this is not the same as receiving Him in fullness and in power. In Ephesians 5:8, Paul declares to a church filled with believers, "Do not be drunk with wine, in which is dissipation; but be filled with the Spirit." Why would Paul issue this command to Christians, unless he perceived it as something significantly different and separate from their conversion experience?

Others have manufactured an outlandish fabrication, arguing that the baptism with the Holy Spirit and the operation of the gifts of the Spirit ended at the death of the last apostle, John, at the end of the first century. First, this idea is located nowhere in the Bible! Second, God has been pouring out His Spirit on believers all over the world for the last two thousand years. According to a Pew Forum analysis of estimates from the Center for the Study of Global Christianity (CSGC) at Gordon-Conwell Theological Seminary, there are about 279 million Pentecostal Christians and 305 million Charismatic Christians in the world. That is a total of 584,080,000 Spirit-filled believers! According to this analysis, Pentecostal and Charismatic Christians together make up about 27 percent of all Christians and more than 8 percent of the world's total population (*http://www.pewforum.org/2011/12/19/global-christianity-movements-and-denominations*). The Pulitzer Center reports that 35,000 people join Pentecostal churches every day. Some researchers predict there will be one billion Pentecostals in the world by 2025.

## Jesus Was Spirit-Filled

The Gospel writer Luke documents that, when Jesus was baptized by John the Baptist, the Holy Spirit descended on Him in "bodily form like a dove" (Luke 3:22). A few verses later, Luke begins chapter 4 with these words: "Then Jesus, being filled with the Holy Spirit, returned from the Jordan." In verse 14, Luke notes, "Then Jesus returned in the power of the Spirit to Galilee." In verse 16-18, he records Jesus attending the synagogue in Nazareth, his hometown. Turning to chapter 61 of Isaiah's prophecy, Jesus read, "The Spirit of the Lord is upon Me, because He has anointed Me." He handed the scroll back to the attendant and said, "Today this Scripture is fulfilled in your hearing" (v. 21).

Clearly, Jesus was filled with the Spirit, saw Himself as anointed by the Spirit, and operated in the power of the Spirit.

Every lesson and sermon Jesus preached, and every healing and miracle He performed, occurred because of the power of the Holy Spirit working through Him. This same Spirit of God and His power are available to you, so you can testify that Jesus is alive and well and working in the world today! The heartbeat of Jesus is that you will be filled, just as He was, and learn to operate in His anointing.

## The Ordinary Has Become the Extraordinary

In the Book of Acts, believers being filled with the Spirit was common. In chapter 2, 120 believers were filled at the initial outpouring of the Holy Spirit on the early church. In chapter 4, many of those same men and women experienced a refilling just a few days later (v. 31). Chapter 8 records how the first non-Jewish believers received the Holy Spirit after Peter and John laid hands on them and prayed for them (vv. 14-17). Cornelius and his family were Gentiles, and they were saved and baptized with the Spirit as Peter preached (ch. 10). In chapter 19, Paul laid his hands on about a dozen former followers of John the Baptist, and the Holy Spirit came upon them (vv. 1-7).

Peter and Paul were full of the Spirit (4:8; 13:9), and the first seven deacons of the early church were baptized with the Holy Spirit (6:3). Barnabas was a recipient of the Holy Spirit (11:24), and a Spirit-filled man named Agabus successfully prophesied of an imminent famine and coming persecution for Paul (11:28; 21:10-11).

I am concerned what was ordinary in the early church has become the extraordinary for many believers today. You may read the Book of Acts and ask, "Can I have what they had? Can I be filled with God's Spirit and minister to people with the supernatural power of God?" The answer is a resounding, "Yes, you can!" What God started in Acts is still available to you right now!

## It's Not Just for Spiritual Super-dupers

Being filled with God's Spirit is not just for preachers and "superspiritual" people. Joel 2:28 proclaims, "It shall come to pass afterward that I will pour out My Spirit on all flesh." This gift is for men and women, old and young people, moms, dads, sons, and daughters. Anyone and everyone who has been born again should be baptized with the Holy Spirit.

You may be wondering, *How can I be filled? What do I have to do?* First, you must *ask Jesus to baptize you* with the Holy Spirit. In Luke 11:13, Jesus told His disciples, "If you then, being evil, know how to give good gifts to your children, how much more will your heavenly Father give the Holy Spirit to those who ask Him!" If I said to you, "I will give you a $100 bill if you will ask me for it," what would you do? You would rush to me immediately and ask for your $100! Jesus has promised the greatest gift (His Spirit in power), and all you have to do is ask Him.

Second, *spend time in praise and worship.* God's presence comes down in glorious ways when we exalt Him. Recently, I was walking through our neighborhood, listening to Christian music. Suddenly, God manifested His presence in me so powerfully that I cried and worshiped as I walked. As you praise the Lord, He will reveal Himself and His glory in your spirit. As an act of faith, thank Him in advance for filling you with His Spirit.

Third, you should *expect to be filled* with the Holy Spirit. Everything you receive from God comes on the wings of your faith. Push out every doubt and fear, and place your trust fully in God and His Word. Hebrews 11:6 asserts, "Without faith it is impossible to please Him, for he who comes to God must believe that He is, and that He is a rewarder of those who diligently seek Him." If God does not fill you the first time you ask Him, be persistent. The disciples waited and prayed for several days before the Spirit was poured out on them, but they prayed with faith repeatedly until God kept His promise!

You may be filled instantly, or you may receive the Holy Spirit infilling after you have prayed awhile. God will determine when He will give you His gift of the Holy Spirit in fullness. Prayer and praise are spiritual activities, and you should not be surprised if you find yourself caught up in the Spirit. You may cry or experience unbelievable joy. However, you will speak in a language you have never learned as the Holy Spirit gives you the words to say.

If you have never been filled with the Spirit, ask Jesus to fill you. Make this a matter of continual prayer until you receive. Talk to God, sharing your heart's desire with Him. Keep it real. My wife was praying with two teenage girls during an altar service in a Church of God youth camp. The girls were saying, "God, You are awesome! You are, like, so unbelievable. You're totally rad!" Leah was amused by their praise, but in a few minutes they were both speaking in tongues as Jesus baptized them with His Holy Spirit!

Read the stories of those who were filled in the Book of Acts (chs. 2, 4, 8, 10, 19). Believe what Peter maintains in 2:38-39: "Repent, and let every one of you be baptized in the name of Jesus Christ for the remission of sins; and you shall receive the gift of the Holy Spirit. For the promise is to you and to your children, and to all who are afar off, as many as the Lord our God will call."

# Speaking in Other Tongues

A FEW YEARS AGO, my friend Mark Brown spent a considerable amount of time in Baton Rouge, Louisiana, due to work. One Sunday, he and a coworker decided to attend a worship service at a Pentecostal church. Mark's friend was not familiar at all with the dynamics of the Holy Spirit, so he was a bit surprised when he heard someone speak in tongues. At lunch, Mark asked his friend, "Well, what do you think about the service and church?" His friend replied, "I liked it. It was different. But I wasn't quite sure about that person speaking in that language. It must be a Cajun thing!"

Mark's friend was wrong and right. Speaking in tongues is not a Cajun thing, but it is different. It is supernatural, and that makes some people uncomfortable. If you have never been exposed to it, the experience can be a little unnerving. Since you serve a supernatural God, however, you should not be surprised if He has chosen to do some supernatural things in you.

## Where It All Began

Speaking in tongues is a New Testament phenomenon that did not occur until fifty days after the death of Jesus Christ. On the Day of Pentecost, 120 believers were baptized with the Holy Spirit for the first time and spoke in tongues (Acts 2). From the context, it seems pretty certain that the eleven apostles, Mary the mother of Jesus, and Jesus' biological brothers were in that group. Speaking in tongues was more than a onetime experience. The rest of the Book of Acts and two thousand years of church history testify it has continued to be the norm for those who are saved and who receive the promised gift of the Holy Spirit.

## Show Some Respect

I confess that I am Spirit-filled and have spoken in tongues many times. Each time I have had this experience, I have walked away humbled and in awe of the overwhelming presence and power of God. However, I cringe in pain and in holy fear when I hear someone criticize or ridicule this operation of the Spirit. I have heard people mock speaking in tongues by uttering gibberish to get a good laugh from an audience. It is not funny, and it is utterly disrespectful. It is treating the holy as something common, and that is sin. I have also listened to others label speaking in tongues as a false doctrine and even call it diabolical.

When I was in college, I worked the evening shift at UPS in Greenville, South Carolina. Several of my coworkers were students at a local ultra-conservative religious university, and we all got along well. One night, I disclosed that I was

Pentecostal. Immediately, these brothers in Christ verbally attacked me, challenging my beliefs. One coworker stared at me coldly and said, "Speaking in tongues is of the devil!" I was eighteen years old and intellectually incapable of defending Pentecost, but I was frightened for that young man. I knew he was bordering on the blasphemy of the Holy Spirit by attributing His work to Satan!

When I was a young teen, my family visited my uncle and his family in Dallas, Texas. My uncle was an accomplished player of any keyboard instrument, and he had been invited to be the guest organist at First Baptist Church of Dallas. The pastor at the time was one of the premier leaders in the Southern Baptist denomination (he has since gone on to be with the Lord), and we were all excited to hear a sermon from one of America's greatest and well-known pastors. As Sunday approached, our excitement grew. We were ready to hear a powerful and encouraging word from the Lord. Instead, to our dismay, his entire message was a diatribe against Pentecostals! My heart was broken as this great man of God, in ignorance, even repeated from the pulpit what my coworker had stated to me at UPS.

The Holy Spirit is the One who enables and inspires anyone to speak in tongues. He is holy, and His work within you is holy. Because He is God, you should always treat Him and His gifts with respect and reverence.

## What Is It?

Speaking in tongues is the God-given ability to speak in a distinct language, unknown to the speaker, as the Holy Spirit enables and inspires him or her to speak. The individual speaks in a language that is not of this world; it is a heavenly language.

In 1 Corinthians 13, often called the Bible's "love chapter," Paul begins with a comment on speaking in tongues: "Though I speak with the tongues of men and of angels, but have not love, I have become sounding brass or a clanging cymbal" (v. 1). Paul strongly implies that he has the ability to speak in the tongues of angels as easily as the known languages of his time. Admittedly, I am guilty of viewing heaven through my American lenses, assuming everyone there speaks English. Clearly, there is a language of heaven, and Paul reveals a believer can speak in that heavenly language—the language of angelic beings. Since Paul spends a considerable amount of space addressing speaking in tongues in chapter 14, he had this in mind when he penned 13:1.

## The Father Gives Good Gifts

A common misconception is that a person goes into a trance and loses control when he or she speaks in tongues. This is not true. People who speak in tongues pray voluntarily, and they can start and stop their prayers whenever they want. Speaking in tongues involves your body and your spirit. Whenever I pray in tongues, it is a spiritual experience. I have learned to sense the Spirit moving in my spirit, and I am keenly aware that He wants to speak through me. Although I am in full control of my faculties, I yield my tongue to Him and speak the words He gives me. He *initiates*, and I *cooperate*.

James 1:17 informs us, "Every good gift and every perfect gift is from above, and comes down from the Father of lights, with whom there is no variation or shadow of turning." Speaking in tongues is a dynamic of God, and it is inherently good. Further, speaking in tongues has been proven to be beneficial to the individual's mind and body. When researchers from the University of Pennsylvania studied speaking in tongues, they discovered it actually produced a feeling of peace and well-being in people who engaged in the behavior. In 2006, *The New York Times* reported that a study of Christians in England suggested that those who speak in tongues are more emotionally stable than those who did not (*http://www .nytimes.com/2006/11/07/health/07 brain.html?_r=0*).

## What's It All About?

Now that we have defined *tongues*, I want us to grasp the purpose of speaking in tongues. There are four divisions in the use of tongues.

1. *Tongues serve as the initial evidence of the baptism with the Holy Spirit.*

I believe you will speak in tongues when you are filled because it occurred (or it is implied that it occurred) in four of the five accounts in Acts. The exception is Paul's infilling in Acts 9, but we know from 1 Corinthians that he spoke in tongues regularly. Tongues serves as the initial (but not the only) evidence that you have been filled.

I am convinced God chose this particular sign for two reasons. First, in the natural, no one utters a language he or she does not know. If you speak in a heavenly language, you will be assured that you have received the Spirit in fullness. Like a guest ringing the doorbell at your home, this is the

Spirit's way of saying to you, "I'm here!" Tongues serve as an indisputable sign that you have been filled with the Spirit.

Second, through the baptism with the Holy Spirit, you enter into the realm of supernatural manifestations. The Spirit-filled believer can flow in the gifts of the Spirit, resulting in healing the sick, performing miracles, and receiving divine revelations about people and situations. To operate in the supernatural, it only makes sense that you begin with the supernatural; that is, by speaking in a language you have never learned.

Repeatedly, I have encountered those who long for the baptism with the Holy Spirit but struggle with the idea of speaking in a language that is not their own. If you are among these, let me reassure you by making this analogy. If you were in a Spanish class in school, you have already spoken in an unknown tongue. Suppose I said to you, "Repeat after me: *El hombre está sentado en la silla* [The man is sitting in the chair]." As you repeated each word, you would be speaking in an unknown tongue or language as I gave you the utterance (the words to say). This is what the Holy Spirit will do for you. He will give you the words to say and, by faith, you will speak them. At that moment, you will be confident that you have been clothed with power from on high!

2. *Tongues serve as a spiritual form of prayer.*

In 1 Corinthians 14:2, Paul discloses, "He who speaks in a tongue does not speak to men but to God." The simplest definition of *prayer* is "speaking to God," so Paul is proposing that speaking in tongues is a form of prayer. Other scriptures support Paul's proposal. Jude 20 reports, "Beloved, building yourselves up on your most holy faith, praying in the Holy Spirit." In Ephesians 6:18, Paul explains spiritual warfare requires the believer "praying always with all prayer and supplication in the Spirit."

Praying in tongues is a special kind of communication because it involves one person of the Godhead (the Holy Spirit) speaking directly to another member (the Father) through you. Paul makes it clear that the person praying in the Spirit "speaks mysteries" (1 Cor. 14:2). While the words are unintelligible to you or to anyone listening, they make perfect sense to God. Now, this begs the question: Can't I just pray in my own language and accomplish the same thing? No. There are benefits in praying in the Spirit that will not occur when you pray in your natural language.

During World War II, Navajo Marines used their native language to relay coded messages (as depicted in the movie *Windtalkers*). The Navajo code was close to unbreakable and so difficult that only a few people could actually learn it. Consequently, this secret code was unintelligible to the enemy. Japanese soldiers intercepted the transmissions, but they could never understand what the Marines were saying.

The devil is the enemy of your soul and is capable of understanding prayers in any human language. If you are struggling with a weakness and you are praying in your native language, the devil can eavesdrop and know everything you are saying. The last thing you want is for your enemy to know your weak spots! When you pray in the Spirit, however, you become a kind of spiritual "windtalker." The devil hears your words, but you are speaking mysteries that only God knows. Romans 8:26 declares, "Likewise the Spirit also helps in our weaknesses. For we do not know what we should pray for as we ought, but the Spirit Himself makes intercession for us with groanings which cannot be uttered." The Spirit tells the Father what you are wrestling with and how you are desperate for help. This leads me to another benefit of praying in tongues.

Paul notes that the person who speaks in a tongue "edifies himself" (1 Cor. 14:4). To *edify* someone is to "build up" or "strengthen." When you pray in the Spirit, God releases divine grace and power so you can overcome your weakness and defeat the Enemy! When I pray in tongues, I am clueless as to what I am saying, but I get up from that experience with peace in my heart and mind. I am assured that God is aware of what I am enduring and everything is going to be all right!

3. *Tongues serve as a spiritual gift.*

This is one of nine gifts of the Spirit (see 1 Cor. 12:8-10), where tongues are spoken aloud in a public gathering of worship and interpreted aloud through the gift of interpretation. According to 14:13, the individual who gives a message in tongues should pray for the interpretation. Two, or at the most three, individuals are permitted to give a message in tongues during the worship service, and each in turn, with someone interpreting each (v. 27). Any attempt by someone to give a fourth message in tongues should be stopped by the pastor immediately. The Spirit will say what He desires through a limited number of speakers.

Incidentally, Paul fails to give any details on the delivery of these gifts. There could be one, two, or three messages in the same service. They could be given consecutively or at various times during the service. It should be noted that messages in tongues are *interpreted*, not *translated*. This would explain why a message in tongues could be lengthy and the interpretation short, or vice-versa. The Holy Spirit is not so much concerned with the construct of the message as He is the content.

I have moderated meetings where two believers were each given a message in tongues. They spoke aloud simultaneously and neither of the individuals would yield to the other. It was very confusing, and I immediately interrupted them. I asked one to wait and directed the other to continue. After the first person finished, I instructed the second person to give their message. I risked being accused of "quenching the Spirit" when I did this, but that was never my intention. If I did not exercise my spiritual authority at that moment, there would have been chaos in the service, and "God is not the author of confusion but of peace" (v. 33).

The gifts of tongues and interpretation serve two distinct purposes. First, they bring an edifying message to the body of Christ. The Holy Spirit uses these gifts and the gift of prophecy to proclaim words that encourage, improve, and instruct the people of God. I have heard it said that prophecy is more valuable than the gift of tongues, but this is not necessarily true. Tongues and interpretation of tongues are equivalent to the gift of prophecy, since an edifying word is delivered to the congregation in a known language. However, without the gift of interpretation, the gift of tongues is unprofitable to anyone in the church. When the gift of tongues is interpreted, the people of God are encouraged and spiritually strengthened (just as they would be with prophecy) because they can understand what they are hearing.

Second, the gift of tongues serves as "a sign . . . to unbelievers" (v. 22). A *sign* is a display used to identify a place of business. If I am driving and want to eat lunch, I look for a restaurant sign. If my gas tank is on empty, I look for a gas station sign. The restaurant and gas station place those signs near the road to get my attention. I have been in services where a sinner was sitting on the back row, completely unengaged in the worship service. The lyrics of the praise choruses or the words of the sermon had no effect on him. Suddenly, someone delivered a message in tongues, and the sinner sat up straight instantly. His eyes were wide open, and he was zoned in on what was happening in the service. The Holy Spirit used the gift of tongues to get that sinner's attention. He realized God was in the house and he needed to get right with the Lord. He tuned in to the message that God was delivering.

A common problem among those who are Spirit-filled is to confuse the prayer language with the gift of tongues. For example, the Spirit will move on an individual to pray in the Spirit, but he thinks it is the gift of tongues. He speaks in tongues loudly and interrupts the service. When he is finished, there is awkward silence. Because it is not the gift of tongues, there is no interpretation, and the church is confused. When this happens, it is the pastor's responsibility to identify the mistake and instruct the one who spoke aloud to be silent— that is, to refrain from interrupting the service anymore. Rather, he should pray to himself quietly to God in the prayer language (v. 28). I recommend the pastor meet with the erring member later to instruct him to differentiate between the *prayer language* and the *gift of tongues*.

How can you know the difference? When the Holy Spirit moves on you to pray, it is intimate and occurs within your personal space. It's a "you" event. However, when you operate in the gift of the Spirit, it is forceful. It is a "group" event. You have an *almost* irresistible urge to speak loud and strong. One of my college professors, Dr. George Voorhis, compared it to having a geyser erupt within you. I must note that the urge is *not* irresistible, since "the spirits of the prophets are subject to the prophets" (v. 32). You can wait until an acceptable moment in the service, instead of interrupting a singer or speaker.

In verse 39, we read, "Do not forbid to speak with tongues." All believers and pastors would do well to heed this apostolic command. Far too many have adopted the philosophy that "If I cannot understand it or control it, I will not permit it." It is natural to fear what one does not comprehend, but Spirit-filled believers should be encouraged, not discouraged, to pray in the Holy Spirit and to operate in all the gifts.

4.  *Tongues serve as foreign languages.*

When this occurs, you speak in a contemporary language which you have never learned. This is what transpired on the Day of Pentecost. Because it was the Feast of Pentecost, Jewish worshipers from all over the world had converged on Jerusalem. After the 120 believers were baptized with the Holy Spirit, the apostles stepped out into the street and spoke in a myriad of languages they had never learned. Acts 2:8 informs us the people heard them speak in their own language in which they were born. The crowd said of the apostles, "Look, are not all these who speak Galileans?" (v. 7). The apostles were from Galilee, and verse 14 says, "Peter, standing up with the eleven," preached the Gospel. God used tongues to get attention, and three thousand souls were saved!

This form of tongues is rare but it still happens today, especially on the mission field. Years ago, I heard the story of a missionary to Japan. He preached in a Pentecostal church, and the altars filled at the conclusion of his message. As he was praying for people, he saw and heard a Japanese woman praising God in perfect English. After the service, he attempted to converse with her, but she could not understand him. Through an interpreter, the missionary informed her that, in the altar, she was speaking in English. In Japanese, she replied, "I was speaking in tongues!" I have been on several mission trips, and the language barrier can be frustrating. Yet, through speaking in tongues, God can bypass the barrier and make it possible for His Word to be proclaimed and His presence to be realized.

## It's Real

Kevin and Renee Summitt are some of our dearest friends in the world. Kevin's great-grandmother was lovingly known as Grandma Butler. She was deaf and mute and could only communicate through sign language. She attended the church where my grandfather, H. D. Sustar, was the pastor. One Sunday, Pappaw Sustar preached on the theme "Being Baptized With the Holy Spirit." As Kevin's grandmother sat by her mom, explaining to her the message in sign language, the Spirit of God came on Grandma Butler. She raised her hands and began speaking in tongues just as anyone with a voice would do. It was a great manifestation of God's ability to do the impossible. After the Spirit ceased speaking, Grandma Butler was again unable to do anything but grunt. From that day forward, when the Spirit blessed her at times, you could hear her glorifying the Father once again in a heavenly language.

Speaking in tongues is real and supernatural. It is a definite work of the Holy Spirit, so you should not resist it. Besides, the main issue is being filled with the Spirit to become a vessel that He can use! If you have not been filled with the Spirit, pray to God for this wonderful blessing. Pray earnestly until you speak in that heavenly language. If you are Spirit-filled, ask God to help you to pray in the Spirit regularly. Also, let Him know you are available and willing to operate in the gift of tongues and interpretation.

# THE GIFTS OF THE SPIRIT

I LOVE READING THE FOUR GOSPELS! I never get tired of reading the stories of Jesus and His ministry. He calmed storms and raging seas. He opened blinded eyes and unstopped deaf ears. He raised the dead and defeated the devil. Once, he had Peter catch a fish that had money in its mouth!

Have you ever read those stories and thought, *Man, I wish I could do what Jesus did!* Guess what? You can! In John 14:12, Jesus announces, "Most assuredly, I say to you, he who believes on Me, the works that I do he will do also; and greater works than these he will do, because I go to My Father." At the Ascension, Jesus returned to His Father and sent the Holy Spirit on the Day of Pentecost to empower His Church to do the works that He did. The Book of Acts records how the Spirit-filled disciples continued the ministry of the Lord with remarkable similarity. When you receive the Spirit in fullness, He empowers you to minister just like Jesus and His disciples ministered through the gifts of the Spirit.

Paul lists nine gifts of the Spirit in 1 Corinthians 12:8-10:

> For to one is given *the word of wisdom* through the Spirit, to another *the word of knowledge* through the same Spirit, to another *faith* by the same Spirit, to another *gifts of healings* by the same Spirit, to another *the working of miracles*, to another *prophecy*, to another *discerning of spirits*, to another *different kinds of tongues*, to another *the interpretation of tongues*.

These nine gifts are available to you from the moment you are baptized with the Holy Spirit.

## Charisma

The word *gift* is *charisma* in the Greek language (the language Paul used when he wrote his letter to the Corinthian church). It means "gift of grace, a free gift, a spiritual endowment, a miraculous faculty." In this sense, to be *charismatic* means to have the gifts of the Spirit functioning in your life or believe these gifts are for the church today.

In 1 Corinthians 12:4-6, Paul discloses, "There are diversities of gifts, but the same Spirit. There are differences of ministries, but the same Lord. And there are diversities of activities, but it is the same God who works all in all." Notice Paul speaks of various kinds of *gifts*, *ministries* and *activities*. Together, these three words define spiritual gifts as "something given to you by God to actively minister to others."

The Holy Spirit gives supernatural gifts to meet the needs of people in and outside church. Paul states, "But the manifestation of the Spirit is given to each one for the profit of all" (v. 7). You never operate in the gifts of the Spirit to have a title, to draw attention to yourself, or to be elevated in the eyes of others. God placed the gifts in the Church for you to minister to hurting and needy people.

The gifts are designed to edify God's people in a worship service and to minister to lost people outside of the church building. Jesus healed the sick not only in synagogues; He healed the sick in the streets, in homes, and in the marketplace. He operated in the gifts of the Spirit, and He wants you to follow His example.

## They Are His Gifts, Not Yours

The gifts spring from the Holy Spirit, not from human resources. The Holy Spirit "works all" of the gifts and distributes them to each person "individually as He wills" (v. 11). If you operate in one of the gifts, you are a vessel through which He manifests that gift.

No one possesses any of the gifts of the Spirit. A person may be used repeatedly in a particular gift, but he cannot lay personal claim to that gift, as though it was his. The gifts are in the Spirit's hands, and He gives them to you at various times as the need demands. This means the Spirit-filled believer has the potential to be used in all nine gifts!

The gifts of the Spirit can be divided into three categories: gifts of revelation, gifts of operation, and gifts of inspiration.

## Gifts of Revelation

Gifts of revelation involve receiving knowledge of some kind from the Holy Spirit. Despite what critics may say, God still speaks to men and women. The very nature of these gifts validates this fact. Scripture and experience indicate that you perceive these Spirit-level communications as spontaneous thoughts, feelings, or impressions.

*The Word of Wisdom.* James 1:5 encourages us to ask God for wisdom if we lack it. The word of wisdom is different. It is when God gives you understanding, direction, or a solution surpassing your mental or intellectual capabilities for a specific situation.

One of the greatest examples of this gift is when some Pharisees challenged Jesus in Matthew 22. Attempting to trick the Lord, they asked Him, "Is it lawful to pay taxes to Caesar, or not?" (v. 17). If Jesus answered "yes," He would lose favor with the Jewish people who despised their Roman captivity. If He answered "no," His enemies would report Him to the Roman authorities as a rebel. Through a word of wisdom, Jesus disarmed His opponents: "Render . . . to Caesar the things that are Caesar's, and to God the things that are God's" (v. 21).

A few months after I planted our church in Anderson, I established a small-group ministry. One of the ladies in our church came to my office and insisted that I make her a small-group leader. I knew this woman was not spiritually qualified to lead a group, but I needed to deny her request without offending her. I prayed under my breath for wisdom. Suddenly, God gave me the words to say that ended the matter with her in a peaceful way. On my own, I never would have conceived my counsel to her.

*The Word of Knowledge.* This is a supernatural revelation of information pertaining to a person or an event that would otherwise not be known. This knowledge is received from the Holy Spirit to enable you to more effectively minister to the needs of people, to know and understand situations, and to effectively combat the tactics of the Enemy. The words you are given bring answers, healing, and understanding.

Jesus operated in this gift when He first met Nathanael (John 1:45-49). Although they had never met each other, the Lord was able to disclose things that Nathanael had said. He even knew where Nathanael was sitting when he said them! Because of this gift, this future apostle was immediately convinced that Jesus was the Son of God.

In Matthew 9, four men brought a paralytic to Jesus for healing. Jesus was divinely aware of the lame man's faith to be saved, and He forgave his sins. When "some of the scribes said within themselves, 'This Man blasphemes'" (v. 3), Jesus knew their thoughts and corrected them (vv. 4-6).

It takes faith and courage to speak a word of knowledge, but I have seen God use this gift in marvelous ways. Once, the pastor of the Calvary Church of God in Westminster, South Carolina, asked me to preach a two-night youth revival. On the first night, I finished preaching and was preparing to give the altar call. Suddenly, the Holy Spirit placed in my mind the silhouette of female organs—like something you would see in a medical journal. The Holy Spirit impressed me that a teenage girl in the congregation had medical problems and that He was going to heal her. Discreetly, I told the congregation what God had shown and told me. Suddenly, a teenage girl (Jessica) and her mother ran to the altar and received prayer. Later, she wrote me a letter explaining she had suffered with serious health problems, and the doctor had told her she would never be able to bear children. After the revival, she went to her OB-GYN for an exam. Her doctor said, "I don't know what has happened to you, but you are fine. There's nothing wrong with you!"

*Discerning of Spirits.* This gift brings the ability to recognize demonic influence and activity. It also allows the believer to have insight into the devilish motives of another person. For example, it could reveal whether a person's sickness was from natural causes or from the devil. Also, this gift protects the church from being infiltrated by demonically controlled individuals who would destroy the local congregation.

One day, Jesus was teaching in one of the synagogues, and there was a woman in the crowd who was "bent over and could in no way raise herself up" (Luke 13:11). It was a serious infirmity, but Jesus discerned that Satan was at the root of her physical problem. For eighteen years this woman had been bound by the devil, but Jesus set her free. She stood straight and gave glory to God (vv. 12-13).

One Sunday, a woman visited our church who was very pushy and, to be quite honest, weird. When I met her, something did not seem right. Immediately, the Spirit let me know that she was a plant of the devil, sent to cause trouble. When she showed up the next Sunday, I confronted her. Realizing I had called her bluff, she stormed from the foyer and never returned.

## Gifts of Operation

These gifts involve direct spiritual activity. You might say they are action gifts. They are designed to enable the church to encounter negative circumstances and effectively counteract or reverse their effect.

*Faith.* This gift activates a supernatural trust and confidence in God in relation to a particular situation. It overrides all of your fear, refuses to succumb to human effort alone, and inspires you to trust God for a mighty work. It replaces panic with peace, in spite of the external circumstances.

In Matthew 8, Jesus and the disciples were in a boat on the Sea of Galilee. An intense storm arose, and their vessel was battered by the waves and swamped with water. The disciples were terrified, but Jesus was in the stern of the boat sleeping. In desperation, they woke Him. With a word, He calmed the storm and asked, "Why are you fearful, O you of little faith?" (v. 26). They had small faith, but Jesus had supernatural faith!

I had never planted a church before, and I had even said that I never would. (Never say "never," because God has a way of proving us wrong!) The thought of starting a new church terrified me. In 1997, God gave me a vision of planting a church in Anderson. In the ensuing months, the Holy Spirit removed my fear of church-planting and gave me a faith that can only be described as supernatural. The gift of faith sustained me as I entered uncharted waters in my ministry. In January 1999, my wife and I moved our family to Anderson to start High Praises Church. Birthing our church would not have been possible without the Spirit activating in me the gift of faith.

*Gifts of Healings.* One of the effects of the curse of sin is that people get ill. By this gift, the Spirit of God miraculously brings healing and deliverance from disease or infirmity. It is significant that Paul writes *gifts of healings* (plural) rather than *gift of healing* (singular). The plural suggests that just as there are many sicknesses and diseases, God has provided a healing for every kind of physical disorder.

The Gospels are replete with stories of Jesus healing by the Spirit. Luke 4:40 says, "All those who had any that were sick with various diseases brought them to Him; and He laid His hands on every one of them and healed them." The same healing virtue that flowed through Jesus can flow through you, bringing healing and health to the sick.

One Sunday, the Holy Spirit was moving powerfully in a service at High Praises, and I was praying for people as they came to the altar with various needs. One of my members, Grace Epps, approached me and asked for prayer. She had a cyst the size of a golf ball on her wrist. I gently laid my hand on the cyst and asked God to heal her. The Holy Spirit sent a gift of healing immediately! When I removed my hand, the cyst was gone and has never returned!

*Working of Miracles.* This is a manifestation of divine power beyond the ordinary course of natural law. You could say that God transcends and bends the laws of nature! If God uses you to perform a miracle, you do something that cannot be done naturally or explained naturally. By definition, a *miracle* is something that only God can do.

Jesus performed a number of miracles. At the wedding of Cana, He turned ordinary water into wine. On the Sea of Galilee, He walked on water and caused Peter to walk on the waves with Him. Twice, He multiplied bread and fish and fed thousands. On three separate occasions, He raised people from the dead.

For two and a half years, our congregation met in a high school. In June 2001, we built a sanctuary on our property. We planned to have our first service in the new building on Father's Day, and we had one week to grade, pave, and stripe the parking lot to get our certificate of occupancy. All week, heavy thunderstorms pounded Anderson County with rain and hail. Yet, not one drop of rain fell on our property! One day that week, I ran outside to see a sheet of rain moving across the tops of the trees and heading straight for our church. Several of my members were in the church. I rushed into the building, informed them what was happening, and asked them to start praying. I ran back outside. Behind our church is a farm pond, and I could see the sheet of heavy rain moving across the water. I cried, "Lord, I need You to stop that rain from coming on this property!" Suddenly, the sheet of rain turned 90 degrees and moved away from the church! The contracted graders and pavers witnessed the whole thing and told everyone, "High Praises is a church that can pray the rain away!"

## Gifts of Inspiration

The inspiration of the Holy Spirit is required for the function of prophecy, tongues, and interpretation of tongues. Because I have dealt with tongues and interpretation previously, I will only deal with the gift of prophecy here.

*Prophecy.* The gift of prophecy is a supernatural and spontaneous utterance in a known language. In the Greek, to *prophesy* means to "speak for another." Consequently, to prophesy is to speak for God! Like the other gifts of the Spirit, it is a divine intervention at a particular moment to meet a pressing need of God's people. The person declaring the prophecy is caught up in the Spirit and, in his own language, speaks a message directly from the heart of God.

Prophecy is not necessarily foretelling the future, although that can be an aspect of any prophecy. It is not the same as preaching, and it is not publicly rebuking the church. Paul gives three purposes for the gift of prophecy: "He who prophesies speaks edification and exhortation and comfort to men" (1 Cor. 14:3). A prophetic word to a local church will strengthen men and women who are weary from spiritual warfare. God will use this gift to call a church in need of revival back to Him. If the church is going through a trial, God will speak words of consolation and support.

To say that Jesus operated in the gift of prophecy would be an understatement! The Lord spoke with divine authority and foretold future events. He *proclaimed* the infallible word of God. At times, He would say, "You have heard that it was said," and He would add, "But I say to you." He *predicted* Peter's denial of Him as well as His own death and His resurrection.

## Don't You Want to Be Used by God?

If you think God saved you to deliver you from hell and take you to heaven, you are only partially correct. Jesus redeemed you to give you abundant life *now*, and that includes working for Him in ministry. Don't you want to be used by God? Does the thought of doing something supernatural through the Holy Spirit appeal to you?

If you are not operating in the gifts of the Spirit, ask Him to flow through you. Tell Him you are a candidate—a vessel He can use. Ask Him to replace any fear with faith and courage. Begin living with the expectation that God is going to use you. Soon, you will know the power and joy of flowing in the gifts of the Spirit!

# WHEN THE NATURAL MEETS THE SUPERNATURAL

THERE IS A NATURAL WORLD, and there is a spiritual world. The natural world is the physical, temporal world around us; the spiritual realm is the invisible (but very real) world of God, angels, and demons. Because you were created a *trichotomy* (spirit, soul, and body), you are able to experience both the natural and the spiritual. Your body, with its five senses, is the gateway to the natural world. Your soul is the gateway to yourself. Your spirit, united and enhanced by the Holy Spirit, is the gateway to God.

The natural and the supernatural worlds often come together for the Spirit-filled saint. Being baptized with the Holy Spirit and operating in the gifts of the Spirit are examples of when these two worlds unite. In each case, God chooses to release and manifest His power through His children to bless them or to bless others through them.

## More Than You Can Stand

Have you ever accidently touched a live electrical wire? It is a shocking experience! I have done it, and I can assure you I did not stand there calmly and say, "My, I am feeling a little something right now." No, I yelled, jerked, and jumped because my body was not designed to handle volts of electricity. Likewise, the power of God surging and flowing in me may cause extraordinary reactions. When the natural meets the supernatural, sometimes, it is more than the natural can stand!

Let's revisit the outpouring of the Holy Spirit on the Day of Pentecost (Acts 2). The recipients of the Spirit were ordinary men and women of all ages. They were intelligent and exhibited good sense. They were Christians—people with sound morals and sound minds. When the Holy Spirit came on them, they appeared to the casual onlooker to be drunkards (vv. 13, 15). They spoke in many languages, which sounded confusing. They possibly reeled, staggered, and fell to the ground, overwhelmed by the presence and power of the Spirit. No one was intoxicated that day; rather, the natural was simply reacting to the supernatural power of God.

## Human Reactions to the Divine

Let's consider four human reactions to the manifestation of the Holy Spirit's presence and power that are often misunderstood and maligned.

*Falling Out Under the Power.* This reaction occurs when someone is so overwhelmed by the presence and the power of the Spirit that they fall to the ground. I have seen this happen countless times, and I myself have fallen under the power several times. I have heard stories of how uninformed people have attended a service where someone fell under the power, and they thought the person had fainted, had a heart attack, or died. They wanted to call 911 and get EMS on the scene!

If you grew up in a Pentecostal church like I did, you may have heard this reaction referred to as being "slain in the Spirit." I do not know where this expression originated, but it can be misleading (especially if you read Acts 5, where Ananias and Sapphira were literally slain by God for their sin!).

The Bible lists three times when sinners were overwhelmed by the power of God and fell to the ground. In John 18:1-8, a mob came to arrest Jesus in the Garden of Gethsemane. He said, "Whom are you seeking?" They answered, "Jesus of Nazareth." The Lord replied, "I am *He*" (vv. 4-5). The word *He* is italicized in the Bible because it was not in the original text. The translators added it for clarity. Jesus actually said, "I am." This is a clear reference to God's revelation of Himself to Moses in Exodus 3:14 as the great "I AM." Jesus was identifying Himself as deity to the armed mob. When He said, "I am," the power and glory of His divinity were released momentarily, and the men "drew back and fell to the ground" (John 18:6). They were overwhelmed by the power of His glory!

The other two examples of sinners falling down are found in Matthew 28:4 and Acts 9:1-4. When the Roman guards at Jesus' tomb witnessed the resurrection of the Lord, they were overcome by that glorious event "and became like dead men." Saul (Paul), the persecutor of the Church, "fell to the ground" when a bright light from heaven shone on him and he heard the voice of Jesus. For tough, religious, hard-hearted Saul, the glory of Christ was more than he could stand!

The prophet Daniel fell twice (Dan. 8:15-18; 10:5-9) and Ezekiel three times (Ezek. 1:26-28; 3:23; 43:3) when they received powerful revelations from the Lord. When the fire of God fell from heaven in 1 Kings 18, the children of Israel fell on their faces and cried, "The Lord, He is God!" (v. 39). In the Revelation, John saw the glorified Christ and confessed, "When I saw Him, I fell at His feet as dead" (1:17).

I have an explanation of why people fall under the power of the Spirit. The Hebrew word for "glory" is *kabod*, which literally means "to be heavy." The glory of God is heavier than the weight of any other glory. You can have moments when the Holy Spirit comes over you with so much of God's presence that you cannot stand under the weight of His glory. You have to yield and fall to the ground.

If you have this happen to you, do not be in a hurry to get to your feet. Lay there and allow the Holy Spirit to minister to you. Ezekiel said the Holy Spirit came on him when he fell. It may be that God will baptize you with the Holy Spirit. Daniel and John received revelations. I would encourage you to lay still and listen for the voice of God. He may speak a powerful word to you!

By the way, I have seen ministers lay hands on people in the altar and literally push them to the floor. This is unacceptable and unnecessary. More than once, I have laid my hand over someone's head without touching them and watched them fall under the power of God. God does not need anyone's help in expressing His glory!

*Running.* Sometimes, when the glory of God touches a child of God, he or she will respond by running quickly and energetically. I have had this happen to me several times. Each time, it occurred as musicians were playing and singing under a powerful anointing from the Holy Spirit. As I was caught up in praising and worshiping the Lord, the glory of

God fell on me so strongly that I could not stay still. I had to run! I ran up and down the aisles of the church, speaking in tongues as I ran.

I know this may sound ludicrous to some of my readers, but continue to read before you label me insane! I can show you in the Scriptures where something similar happened to a man of God. In 1 Kings 18, Elijah had a showdown with the prophets of the false god Baal. After preparing a sacrifice on the altar, the old prophet prayed down fire from heaven. It consumed the sacrifice and the altar, and this supernatural manifestation turned the hearts of the people back to Jehovah.

At the conclusion of this event, Elijah received a word from the Lord. For three and a half years, it had not rained in Israel. The drought, however, was coming to an end, and God was going to send rain once again on the land. King Ahab had come to watch the confrontation between Elijah and the false prophets, and Elijah told him to head back to the city of Jezreel at once because there was "the sound of abundance of rain" (v. 41). Ahab did not have to be told twice. If the man of God could pray down fire from heaven, he could pray down rain, too!

The king departed for Jezreel immediately in his chariot. I imagine the king had the fastest horses in the land, and his chariot driver loosened the reins on those steeds. Suddenly, something extraordinary happened. King Ahab caught something out of the corner of his eye, and to his amazement, he saw the prophet Elijah. The Bible says, "Then the hand of the Lord came upon Elijah; and he girded up his loins and ran ahead of Ahab to the entrance of Jezreel" (v. 46). Friend, if the hand of God touches you, do not be surprised if a spirit of running comes on you like it did on Elijah!

*Dancing.* When I mention dancing, what comes to your mind? Night clubs? Frat parties? The latest pop singer gyrating on stage? For many, dancing is a secular activity that could never be done in a spiritual way. Some would argue that dancing has no place in praise and worship, but the Bible would disagree. Ecclesiastes 3:1, 4 says, "To everything there is a season, a time for every purpose under heaven . . . a time to mourn, and a time to dance." The psalmist declares, "Let them praise His name with the dance" (Ps. 149:3) and "Praise Him with the timbrel and dance" (150:4).

People dance to celebrate. At most wedding receptions, dancing is part of the festivities. A DJ is playing music, and the wedding party and guests are on the dance floor. Everyone is having fun because a wedding is a joyous occasion. It is party time!

Getting in the presence of Jesus is a joyous event. I feel joy that is unspeakable and full of glory! Psalm 16:11 states, "In Your presence is fullness of joy; at Your right hand are pleasures forevermore." When I am filled with the joy of the Lord, I have discovered I can dance before the Lord. I do not try to do the electric slide or the cupid shuffle! Instead, I do my own dance in a holy and spiritual form of praise and worship.

When David brought the ark of the covenant into Jerusalem, it was a spiritual party. Second Samuel 6:12 depicts the Israelites bringing up the ark "with gladness." Thousands offered sacrifices to the Lord in the prescribed form of worship according to the Law. Music was playing, and everyone was singing. The atmosphere was electrified. Suddenly, King David shocked everyone. He removed his royal diadem and robes. He laid aside everything that would draw attention to him and would get in the way of his worship. Verse 14 says David "danced before the Lord with all his might."

The Hebrew word for "danced" suggests David did not do a dignified waltz. Rather, he spun around wildly, with his arms outstretched! What would cause a king to put on such a scandalous public display? It was the presence and power of God generating joy and excitement deep within David's being. The King of all kings was David's God, and this truth was more than he could stand. He had to dance!

When you feel the overwhelming joy of God's presence, you have a right to express yourself in spiritual worship in dance. If all you can do is bounce up and down or jump, take your liberty and praise your Savior! The only thing that will stop you is being self-conscious or worrying about what others may think of you. If self-consciousness keeps you from worshiping, you have the sin of pride in your heart. If you are consumed and controlled by the opinions of others, you are in bondage to fear. Refuse to permit pride and fear to bind up your worship. Remove those things that hinder your worship and dance before the Lord with every ounce of your strength!

*Shouting.* Somewhere along the way, someone came up with the idea that all church services should be quiet and reverent. No one should say anything except the person standing on the platform. Unless there is a responsive reading or the singing of a hymn, congregants are supposed to keep their mouth shut.

Once, I attended a church like that. When the pastor made a really good point, I quietly said aloud, "That's good preaching!" My wife almost elbowed me. She told me later that it sounded to her like I had yelled my words, even though I had not.

When I read my Bible, I understand it is OK to be expressive in church. There are moments when it is appropriate to shout and make some noise! By *shouting*, I mean issuing a shout of joy, a cry of jubilee, or a victory shout. We raise our voice and let loose praise and worship. It is saying things like, "Hallelujah! Glory! Thank You, Jesus! Amen!" Once, when preaching to an African-American congregation, I declared a powerful spiritual truth, and a woman stood up and shouted, "Oh, that's nasty, Pastor!"

The Bible contains several examples of God's people shouting to the Lord. In Joshua 6, when the walls of Jericho fell supernaturally, "the people shouted with a great shout" (v. 20). Ezra 3:11 tells us when Israel began restoring the Temple, "all the people shouted with a great shout, when they praised the Lord, because the foundation of the house of the Lord was laid." Remember the story of David bringing the ark of the covenant into the city of Jerusalem? While David danced before the Lord with all his might, 2 Samuel 6:15 says Israel "brought up the ark of the Lord with shouting and with the sound of the trumpet."

I love the Psalms, but sometimes I forget they are songs that were used in worship. Through their lyrics, the psalmists encouraged the people of God to lift their voices high and loud in praise.

- "Oh, clap your hands, all you peoples! *Shout* to God with the voice of triumph!" (47:1).

- "Oh come, let us sing to the Lord! Let us *shout* joyfully to the Rock of our salvation. Let us come before His presence with thanksgiving; let us *shout* joyfully to Him with psalms" (95:1-2).

- "*Shout* joyfully to the Lord, all the earth; break forth in song, rejoice, and sing praises" (98:4).

- "Make a joyful *shout* to the Lord, all you lands! Serve the Lord with gladness; come before His presence with singing" (100:1).

There is a connection between spiritual gladness, singing, and shouting. I love to be in a worship service where someone is singing under the anointing, and the Spirit of God is speaking words of victory and joy to the congregation. The next thing you know, people are shouting aloud, standing up, lifting their hands, and jumping for joy! I usually join them!

I have a member at High Praises named Charlie Brown. Yep, Charlie Brown attends my church! He and his wife, Shirley, were saved shortly after they started attending our services. My brother-in-law, Joel Talley, is an evangelist who is used mightily by the Spirit. I had him come preach a revival, and Charlie attended each service. Joel normally lays hands on people in the altar service, and most of the people he prays for fall under the power of God. He has that kind of anointing flowing through him. Charlie watched Joel with great skepticism. He said, "That's not real" . . . until Joel asked Charlie if he could pray for him. Charlie agreed, and Joel gently laid his hand on his head. Immediately, Charlie fell to the floor. Later, when I asked him about the experience, he said, "I was a doubter before, but not anymore. It is real, and I want more!" What happened to Charlie Brown? The natural met the supernatural. When the natural meets the supernatural, sometimes it is more than the natural can stand!

What about you? Does the idea of being overwhelmed by the power of God scare you or excite you? Are you critical about running, dancing or shouting in church, or are you hungry to be set free in your praise and worship? I am not talking about sheer emotionalism; I am referring to spiritual worship. "God is Spirit, and those who worship Him must worship in spirit and truth" (John 4:24).

I hope these words will persuade you to pray for experiences that will fuse your natural world with the spiritual world. Ask the Holy Spirit to deliver you from fear or apprehension. Tell Him you want more! He will answer your prayer, so get ready. When He does, you will know firsthand what Paul meant when he said, "Where the Spirit of the Lord is, there is liberty" (2 Cor. 3:17).

# Conclusion

A BOY STOOD ON A WINDY HILLSIDE, flying a kite. As he continued to release the string of the kite, it went higher and higher until it was completely out of sight. One of his friends walked up and asked how he knew there was still a kite on the other end. He replied, "I know it's there; I feel it tugging on the line."

The Holy Spirit is like the boy's kite. You cannot see Him, but you know He is present by His work in your life. If you are a sinner, you feel Him tugging at your heart with conviction and love to come to Christ and be saved from your sins. If you are born again, He tugs at you daily to make right moral choices that please your heavenly Father or to walk in faith during a trial. If you are Spirit-filled, you experience His tug in your spirit to speak in a heavenly language or operate in His gifts.

The spiritual tugs are what make living for Jesus so exciting! He will open an opportunity for you to share Jesus with someone at work, or call you to volunteer at your church in a ministry. He will lead you into incredible peace and assurance in the midst of a major crisis, or free you to shout and rejoice while engaged in spiritual warfare. He will give you the right words to say when your son asks you a difficult spiritual question. He might even perform a miracle through you.

Greg McDuffie sings in the choir at High Praises Church and has served as a deacon. He has a magnetic personality and can tell some of the funniest stories. He is also a man of tremendous faith and godliness. Last year, Greg had a medical exam and was devastated to learn he had a tumor in him the size of a football. All tests indicated it was attached to his organs and tissues, and one doctor plainly told him he was in serious trouble. Greg was scheduled to have surgery at Emory Hospital in Atlanta, Georgia, and the doctors informed him it would be a long and complicated procedure.

The Sunday before his surgery, God's Spirit directed one of my members, James Whittington, to go to the choir and pray for Greg. I was preaching, but James obeyed the Lord. He walked right past me, walked up to Greg, and said, "The Lord has told me to pray for you." As he prayed, the Holy Spirit came on Greg in supernatural power, and Greg began speaking in tongues. He knew God had done something in his body. When he sat down after the prayer, God spoke to him and said, "I have prepared you for surgery." At that moment, a lasting peace settled on Greg.

A few days later, when the doctors performed his surgery, they were shocked to see the tumor completely detached from any organs or tissues. The tumor was quickly removed without any of the expected complications, and Greg was out of surgery in no time. It was nothing short of a miracle, and the doctors said so. Later, James told us he had no idea Greg had a tumor or was going to have surgery. Because he simply obeyed the Spirit's tug, the *natural* met the *supernatural* in Greg's body.

The God who performed that miracle is living inside of you in the person of the Holy Spirit. Yield to His divine tugs and live in the Spirit every day. Those tugs will lead to your own personal testimony of the presence and power of the Holy Spirit.

# Acknowledgments

With deep appreciation, I acknowledge the support and guidance of the following people who helped make this book possible:

Hats off to the faithful members of the High Praises Church of God.

Special thanks to Wanda Knight for her invaluable critique of the manuscript.

I'm grateful for the advice and guidance from my father, T. David Sustar, who is an accomplished author and the best dad in the world.

And finally, I'm indebted to my wife, Leah, and my wonderful and supportive family.

—Chris Sustar